£10·25
1c95

7

PRAC
SOCIAL

D0756648

Series Editor: Jo Campling

BASW

Social work is at an important stage in its development. All professions must be responsive to changing social and economic conditions if they are to meet the needs of those they serve. This series focuses on sound practice and the specific contribution which social workers can make to the well-being of our society.

The British Association of Social Workers has always been conscious of its role in setting guidelines for practice and in seeking to raise professional standards. The conception of the Practical Social Work series arose from a survey of BASW members to discover where they, the practitioners in social work, felt there was the most need for new literature. The response was overwhelming and enthusiastic, and the result is a carefully planned, coherent series of books. The emphasis is firmly on practice set in a theoretical framework. The books will inform, stimulate and promote discussion, thus adding to the further development of skills and high professional standards. All the authors are practitioners and teachers of social work representing a wide variety of experience.

JO CAMPLING

A list of published titles in this series follows overleaf

PRACTICAL SOCIAL WORK

Self-Help, Social Work and Empowerment
Robert Adams

Social Work and Mental Handicap
David Anderson

Beyond Casework
James G. Barber

Practising Social Work Law
Suzy Braye and Michael Preston-Shoot

Citizen Involvement: A Practical Guide for Change
Peter Beresford and Suzy Croft

Social Workers at Risk
Robert Brown, Stanley Bute and Peter Ford

Social Work and Mental Illness
Alan Butler and Colin Pritchard

Social Work and Europe
Crescy Cannan, Lynne Berry and Karen Lyons

Residential Work
Roger Clough

Social Work and Child Abuse
David M. Cooper and David Ball

Management in Social Work
Veronica Coulshed

Social Work Practice: An Introduction
Veronica Coulshed

Social Work and Local Politics
Paul Daniel and John Wheeler

Sociology in Social Work Practice
Peter R. Day

Anti-Racist Social Work: A Challenge for White Practitioners and Educators
Lena Dominelli

Working with Abused Children
Celia Doyle

Applied Research for Better Practice
Angela Everitt, Pauline Hardiker, Jane Littlewood and Audrey Mullender

Welfare Rights Work in Social Services
Geoff Fimister

Student Supervision in Social Work
Kathy Ford and Alan Jones

Working with Rural Communities
David Francis and Paul Henderson

Children, their Families and the Law
Michael D. A. Freeman

Family Work with Elderly People
Alison Froggatt

Child Sexual Abuse
Danya Glaser and Stephen Frosh

Computers in Social Work
Bryan Glastonbury

Working with Families
Gill Gorell Barnes

Women, Management and Care
Cordelia Grimwood and Ruth Popplestone

Women and Social Work: Towards a Woman-centred Practice
Jalna Hanmer and Daphne Statham

Youth Work
Tony Jeffs and Mark Smith (eds)

Problems of Childhood and Adolescence
Michael Kerfoot and Alan Butler

Social Work with Old People
Mary Marshall

Applied Psychology for Social Workers
Paula Nicolson and Rowan Bayne

Crisis Intervention in Social Services
Kieran O'Hagan

Social Work with Disabled People
Michael Oliver

Separation, Divorce and Families
Lisa Parkinson

Social Care in the Community
Malcolm Payne

Working in Teams
Malcolm Payne

Working with Young Offenders
John Pitts

Effective Groupwork
Michael Preston-Shoot

Adoption and Fostering: Why and How
Carole R. Smith

Social Work with the Dying and Bereaved
Carole R. Smith

Child Care and the Courts
Carole R. Smith, Mary T. Lane and Terry Walsh

Social Work and Housing
Gill Stewart and John Stewart

Anti-Discriminatory Practice
Neil Thompson

Community Work
Alan Twelvetrees

Working with Offenders
Hilary Walker and Bill Beaumont (eds)

Citizen Involvement

A Practical Guide for Change

Peter Beresford

and

Suzy Croft

MACMILLAN

First published 1993 by
THE MACMILLAN PRESS LTD
Houndmills, Basingstoke, Hampshire RG21 2XS
and London
Companies and representatives
throughout the world

ISBN 0-333-48300-6 hardcover
ISBN 0-333-48301-4 paperback

A catalogue record for this book
is available from the British Library.

Copy-edited and typeset by Povey-Edmondson
Okehampton and Rochdale, England

Printed in Hong Kong

Series Standing Order (Practical Social Work)

If you would like to receive future titles in this series as they are
published, you can make use of our standing order facility. To
place a standing order please contact your bookseller or, in case
of difficulty, write to us at the address below with your name and
address and the name of the series. Please state with which title
you wish to begin your standing order. (If you live outside the
UK we may not have the rights for your area, in which case we
will forward your order to the publisher concerned.)

Standing Order Service, Macmillan Distribution Ltd,
Houndmills, Basingstoke, Hampshire, RG21 2XS, England

In loving memory of my mother, Ida Beresford (née Kaufman), 1909–90, and our neighbour, Dot Lucas, 1910–89, who bore witness that it is as important for people to be empowered at the end of their life as during the course of it

Contents

Acknowledgements   viii

Introduction   x

1 **Making Sense of Citizen Involvement**   1

2 **First Steps to Involvement: Information-Gathering
   and Consultation**   23

3 **From More Responsive Services to a Direct Say in
   Decision-Making**   42

4 **Key Components for Effective Involvement**   60

5 **Guidelines for Involvement: The Agency
   Perspective**   92

6 **Getting Involved with Other People: Moving from
   Individual to Collective Action**   113

7 **Guidelines for Involvement: Empowering Ourselves**   128

8 **Guidelines for Involvement: Developing an
   Empowering Practice as Workers**   157

9 **Towards a Policy for Citizen Involvement**   177

*A Framework for Evaluating Citizen Involvement in
Agencies and Services*   205

Further Reading   221

Index   229

Acknowledgements

We have many people to thank. Our first thanks must go the the Joseph Rowntree Foundation which made it possible for us to carry out the three-year research project on citizen involvement upon which this book draws. We also have a debt to the King's Fund and British Association of Social Workers for the additional support they offered.

In our research, we aimed to explore a wide range of participatory initiatives. We did this as systematically as possible, first through our own networks and grapevine, then by advertising widely through posters, leaflets, newsletters and articles and finally by making a national survey of statutory and voluntary services. We had a large response from all kinds of projects, from a development worker bringing together hearing impaired people to try and communicate their needs to their neighbourhoods and services and an advocacy project for parents of school children with learning difficulties, to a department initiating annual plans in decentralised districts which included consultation with service users and a council day nursery setting up a parents' committee. We made direct contact with more than eighty innovatory schemes and initiatives and the people involved in them. We want to thank all of them for giving us their help.

When we asked for people's help in our research, many contacted us asking for *ours*. We heard from workers, isolated and unaware of developments elsewhere, set what sounded like impossible tasks by their agencies. We spoke to service users sometimes left wondering if they were just being awkward customers because they wanted more control over their lives. Occasionally we have had the same feeling ourselves!

We want to offer our particular thanks to people involved in rights movements and service user organisations. These are almost invariably overstretched and lacking adequate resources, so their help is especially valued. We hope this book helps repay it.

We wanted the process of producing this book to be as participatory as its subject. We should like to thank the people involved in participatory initiatives who read a first draft for the many helpful changes and improvements their comments and ideas have made possible.

Finally we should like to thank Alan Stanton for his unstinting help, Jo Campling for her commitment to this book, and Maggie Hilton for the support she has given us.

We have learnt many things during the course of this work. We have forged new links, met impressive people and projects and gained fresh insights into people's empowerment. Writing this book has been an empowering experience for us. We hope reading it will be for other people.

PETER BERESFORD
SUZY CROFT

Introduction

A powerful idea is gaining ground. People have a right to a say and involvement in the services they use, in the neighbourhoods where they live and in the institutions that affect them. The aim of policy should be to increase people's participation, not to inhibit it. We should all be able to take control of our lives and make real choices. Whatever our age, race, sex or status, we are entitled to be ourselves, to be accepted for what we are and not devalued or subject to discrimination.

The question is no longer whether people *should* have a voice in local life and services, but *how* this is to be achieved. It is not just the promise of greater citizen involvement that's now needed, but ways of realising it. It's time to move from rhetoric to reality. The aim of this book is to help make that possible. It is intended as both an introduction and a guide to citizen involvement.

The background to this book

We don't start from a blank page. Much has already been done. Work to encourage people's participation has been going on for years, quietly and unfêted, in mainstream services as well as pioneering projects. There is a body of knowledge to be built on – if we can find it. But such experience is frequently inaccessible, unrecorded, lost. People involved in innovatory initiatives often don't have the time or confidence to write about them. Those on the receiving end are even less likely to have had the chance to put pen to paper.

x

Expert accounts are sometimes too far removed from the reality to be helpful. As a result, most of us, whether we work in organisations and services or use them, still have little idea how to gain a greater say in them. We neither know what's possible nor what problems to expect.

The two of us have been fortunate. We have had the rare opportunity to meet and talk with a wide range of people involved as service users and workers in initiatives to involve and empower people in Britain. We have been able to find out more about work going on in other countries. We have also drawn on our own experience in community action, as users of social services, income maintenance, housing benefit and other stigmatising services, and through our continued involvement in rights and user groups and initiatives. These have ranged from an international tribunal for poor women, to a meeting bringing together disabled people, people with learning difficulties and people with mental distress to exchange experience and explore possibilities for common action. One of us (Suzy) works part-time as a qualified social worker in a multidisciplinary support team with people with cancer, their families and friends, and can also draw on this experience of trying to work in a participatory and empowering way. All this has offered us insights and access we might not otherwise have had, helped us keep our feet firmly on the ground and made it possible to write from our own as well as from many other people's first hand experience.

Our personal concern with increasing people's involvement and empowerment goes back to 1977. But recent social, political and economic changes have led to an accelerated interest in involvement. It's now much higher on official agendas. New windows have opened for it. This book is both a reflection of that and an attempt to take the issue forward.

The book focuses particularly on citizen involvement in social work and social services, but we have also explored initiatives in other fields like housing, health, education, youth and community work, land-use planning and self-help initiatives. All have helpful lessons to offer. Such cross-fertilisation is invaluable, but it doesn't often happen. Schools try to involve parents as school governors, unaware of the lessons learned by community workers. Hospitals consult patients oblivious of the experience of community architects. Yet efforts to involve people confront similar issues whatever their context. We face the same problems whether we are trying to see our medical records, get better street cleaning or make a complaint at the local supermarket. Services like social work raise these issues with particular intensity because they are so closely involved with questions of personal rights, responsibility and freedom. They can remove our children, place us in institutions and restrain our physical liberty.

We have placed a particular emphasis in this book on the perspective of service users and other people who have experience of participatory schemes or have perhaps set up their own. This doesn't mean we discount the viewpoints of others, like practitioners, managers and politicians. They will also be heard here. But people on the receiving end have a special significance. They usually have the fewest opportunities to put their side of the story. Yet who knows better than they whether attempts to involve and empower people are actually effective?

In our discussions with people, we have tried to find out what works and what doesn't, what skills they need and how they have gained them. We have talked about the problems they have met and how they have overcome them. How did you get started? How do new people get involved? What does 'getting involved' actually entail? What do you feel you have been able to achieve? How do you deal with racism, sexism and other oppressions?

One point we should stress at the start. Gaining a greater say and involvement is something that concerns *all of us*. It's not just other people's problem, even though some groups are particularly powerless. We may only realise this when something goes wrong, our circumstances change or we come into collision with an official agency. There may be times when we are more vulnerable to outside control, for example, when we are older or unemployed, but these can happen to anyone. Then we may suddenly see how easily we are excluded and how little we can do about it.

The aims of this book

We have tried to pull together ideas, information and experience. This book draws on participatory initiatives we have followed up. It's illustrated by people's own comments. It doesn't tell a simple success story. There are probably more failures than successes, but lessons can be learned from both. Few schemes have got everything right. There aren't many models of good practice, but we can all begin to tease out our own from the wealth of work already being done. We are not offering any grand theory here, but we hope readers will find a set of guidelines, principles and values which make sense and are helpful.

The purpose of this book is to support people trying to increase their own and other people's say and involvement. We have found that people learn best by doing, not by reading! This book is intended to fit into that process of reflection and action. It's not meant to replace people's experience, but to help inform and make sense of it. Readers will be able to compare their own experience with other people's, draw on developments from a wide range of different fields and see some of the traps you can fall into. We have tried to avoid being prescriptive. We aren't saying you must do it this way or it only works like that. We describe a range of different approaches to involvement. Readers can make their own choices about how they get involved or support other people's involvement.

Some people may choose to read the book from beginning to end. For others there may be particular things they want to know more about now. Some readers may want to turn first to find out how they might gain more say for themselves. Others may be most interested in how they as workers can help empower others. We have tried to organise the book so that people can use it either way: dipping in or reading it right through.

Perhaps we should also say what this book is *not*. It's not a guide to current initiatives to involve people or gain more say. It does not offer a series of case studies. Such a book is unlikely to be helpful. It will be out of date before it's even completed. Initiatives come and go. They change. They have their good and bad times. Preserving them on paper will only distort them and deceive us. That is one reason why we haven't identified specific initiatives by name. Another is to preserve the anonymity of those which were having problems. We have tried to go beyond the well-worn paths of showpiece projects while at the same time avoiding the creation of new legends to add to the many that already abound. We don't want to set people off on more pilgrimages.

Though the emphasis here is practical, we have tried to identify principles and offer guidelines. We won't be ignoring or denying the key political, philosophical and theoretical issues that participation raises. Perhaps the reluctance to acknowledge these in the past has been one of the reasons for its many failings.

There are two audiences we particularly hope this book will help: people involved in community, disability, service users' and carers' organisations, and agencies and workers committed to increasing people's involvement and say. They are likely to come to it with very different experiences, expectations and agendas. This book reflects that. It explores the issues of policy and practice facing agencies and services as well as the personal and organisational issues we must all address if we are to have more say in them. Setting these side by side may bring another benefit. By offering each group an introduction to the needs and perspective of the other it may help both learn how progress can best be made.

When we explained what we were doing to one user group and asked for their help, one member said: 'If we talk about how we do things, if that's written down, then services who want to will know how to block us.' He may have a point, but as we said to him, 'How will other people who want to get involved, be able to effectively, if experience isn't shared?' A development worker involved in an older women's group said, 'I was involved in tenants' groups in the seventies. There were lots of handbooks for tenants' action. None of them was any good. The tenants' movement was not a success.' We might not accept her final judgement, but she is right to warn us against having too high expectations of handbooks. They can only offer a starting point. They may only reach people who are already organised and involved. But that's still important.

Before we turn to the structure of the book, a word about terminology. There is no agreed language in this field. Instead there is now talk of 'consumer choice', 'user involvement', 'customers' and 'participation'. Each can mean different things to different people and most are offensive to somebody. As one man with experience of psychiatric services said, 'People who use mental health services are no more consumers of them than wood lice are of Rentokil.' It's an issue we'll come back to later. At the risk of coining yet more jargon, we prefer the term *citizen involvement*. It emphasises people's civil status, isn't tied to any particular philosophy and doesn't define them in terms of the services they use.

The structure of the book

This book is organised according to the themes and issues which emerge from existing experience and initiatives to involve people. It is concerned with three key questions: why greater citizen say and involvement? what is it? and how is it to be achieved? The last of these is the book's theme, but in Chapter 1 we offer an introduction to the first two. We try to clarify what getting involved means, put it in a broader philosophical and theoretical context, examine why there is such interest in it now and consider some of the questions that have been raised about it.

Chapter 2 begins to look at people's involvement in practice. We focus on the two most widely used approaches, information-gathering and consultation. How do you do it? What are the practicalities and problems?

Chapter 3 moves on to some of the wider issues these raise. It introduces the idea of empowerment and people having a direct say in decision-making. It looks first at the issue of equipping people to have a say. What skills and support do we need? How can we get them? In Chapter 4 we look at what the key components of such involvement and empowerment might be, from information to training, advocacy to access. Chapter 5 offers a set of practical guidelines for citizen involvement based on people's experience in a wide range of settings.

Chapter 6 takes us from individual involvement to collective action. What are their different strengths and weaknesses? We pay particular attention to community development approaches to involving people in local life and services, considering both their pitfalls and possibilities and offering guidelines for positive practice.

Chapter 7 outlines a process of empowerment from the viewpoint of people seeking more say themselves. What steps must we take to have more control over our lives and services? How do we move from our personal needs to having a direct say in public policy? How can we work with other people to achieve change? We look at components of this process: developing first hand accounts, learning to work together, forming our own judgements, negotiating our decisions, taking part in broader debates, running our own services.

Finally, Chapters 8 and 9 take us back to the perspective of agencies and their workers, looking first at how they can develop a more open and empowering practice and then exploring a policy for citizen involvement. Chapter 9 offers a checklist to help make that possible and to audit involvement. This also provides readers with a guide to the book, showing them where they can find more detailed discussion of particular issues and areas of citizen involvement.

The centrality of citizen involvement

Our concern may be with better services, individual rights, public accountability or democratisation. We may see them as four very different approaches. But people's involvement is central to them all. Without it, accountability can only be upward or indirect. Democracy that isn't participatory can feel very far away. How will we gain our rights if we have no say in them? How can services that exclude people be sensitive to their needs?

Once we start talking about involving' people, a constellation of words recurs, words like 'say', 'control' and 'empowerment'. That's because the issue is crucially about

taking control over our lives, the services we use, our environment and the political worlds in which we live. It's not likely
to be easy for any of us. For women and people who are poor,
disabled or facing other discrimination, the difficulties will
probably be that much greater. Participation can also be
divisive, setting one group against another.

At the same time, it can bring us together. Instead of being
fragmented in single-issue campaigns, participation can unite
us in an understanding of the difficulties we share from being
excluded or ignored. It also emphasises our common ground
as service providers and users. We may be drawn to participation by different motives: the practitioner who wants to work
in more equal and accessible ways, the citizen who is no
longer prepared to be oppressed by an overpowering agency.
But it can offer benefits to both.

Major changes are now taking place in public services.
There is increasing interest in Britain and elsewhere in a
changed economy of care. The search is on for a different
balance of provision between the public, commercial and not-
for-profit sectors. We have seen participatory initiatives in all
three, but just changing the source of supply doesn't necessarily bring people's involvement any closer. No sector has
shown a particular capacity to offer such involvement. The
question of how to increase citizen say and involvement faces
all services whoever provides them. The sea-changes in public
services and utilities we are now seeing only emphasise the
scale and urgency of the task facing us.

We would like this book to offer inspiration, ideas and
practical help to people who are trying to get involved
themselves or to empower others. We hope it will encourage
others to try too. Then it may serve as the book we needed
but never had when we first got involved. With many small
steps like this, there's a real chance that people's involvement
in their neighbourhoods and services can become the day-to-
day reality which our assumptions that we live in a democracy
suggest it should be.

1
Making Sense of Citizen Involvement

What say do you feel *you* have in your neighbourhood and the services you use? For most people it seems to be little or none. That's been the message from our own and other research for more than 15 years, from inner city tower blocks to leafy suburban semis.

> **'There's nothing in it for me. They take no notice of us.'**

> **'If I talk from here to breakfast time, no one will listen. If they listened to us it would be OK.'**

Five years, and governments and councils at opposite ends of the political spectrum, separate these comments, but it's a similar story. Whether people are old or young, black or white, women or men, they largely feel powerless and excluded (Beresford and Croft, 1978, 1986).

On the other hand, if we do get involved, it may be a shattering experience that changes our lives. It can transform the way we see ourselves and the world in which we live. As a disabled woman said to us:

> **'I went to this meeting on disability. I heard a lot of people saying things that I had thought myself but never said. I'd never put them into words myself. I was terrified when I first got involved. I never thought I'd be able to do things like speak publicly and have the confidence to do things that other**

1

people were doing. But I've built up the skills and confidence I needed, always with help from other people. Getting involved has changed me. I am different now.'

Whether we are trying to gain compensation, struggling to get appropriate services for ourselves or someone else, challenging local redevelopment plans, campaigning for a new amenity, or taking up the cudgels over a miscarriage of justice, the effect may be the same. What began as a chance intervention may become a life's work. Our eyes are opened. There may be much pain as well as gain. It is a milestone in our lives.

Why the interest in citizen involvement?

Involving people can clearly have profound effects for us all. It is not something to be embarked upon lightly. Yet there has been an explosion of enthusiasm for it. Politicians of the left, right and centre all sing its praises. It's become an essential ingredient of a growing number of official reports. The desire for more say in services has extended from the police to public transport. You are almost as likely to hear central government representatives as local community activists arguing the importance of 'bottom-up' initiatives. Why this interest?

It comes from many quarters and there are many reasons, but most can be traced to disenchantment with the British postwar welfare state. The 1980s saw it judged and found wanting. The political right attacked it for its inefficiency, expense and creation of dependency. State services were called into question, first because of recession and reduced resources and then by ideological arguments for a new social economy with a much greater emphasis on the market place.

At the same time, new, assertive organisations and movements of people who used services emerged, ranging from young people in care to people with mental distress. They rejected the poor quality, paternalism and social control of welfare services. They argued that services should enable people to decide things for themselves instead of doing things to or for them. They began to demand something different. There was support for this from the other side of the counter, from people who wanted to work in different, more participatory ways. Moves to more decentralised and community-orientated services gave added impetus to ideas of user and local involvement.

New kinds of services appeared. By showing that things really could be different, they emphasised the deficiencies of the old. Women's organisations and gay women and men, for example, set up lesbian lines, rape crisis centres and buddy schemes. These established different relationships between service users and providers, met needs that had previously been ignored and were often run in more collaborative ways.

New philosophies emerged that gave greater force and focus to ideas of citizen involvement. The theory of 'social role valorisation' or 'normalisation' as it was first called, with its emphasis on social integration and a valued life for people, provided a participatory framework, first for people with learning difficulties and then for other groups. It has come in for criticism for its association with dominant values and ideas of normality in society, but participation is a crucial element in the five 'accomplishments' it identified for effective services. These are:

● community presence
● protecting rights and promoting choice
● recognising interests and gifts; improving competence
● promoting valued roles
● community participation (O'Brien and Tyne, 1981; O'Brien and Lyle, 1987).

Disabled people developed a new politics of disability based on a critique of existing services, a redefinition of the problem and an attempt to create an alternative service structure controlled by disabled people themselves. This followed from a social model of disability which emphasises that people's disability is caused by social factors, not by their individual impairments. What disables people is their inability to function in an able-body orientated world which does not take account of their rights and needs.

Ideas of involvement and empowerment have been given added force by broader developments in society. They reflect the renewed concern in the late 1980s with issues of citizenship and the rights and responsibilities that go with it in a democratic society. They echo the demands of women and members of minority ethnic groups for equal say and opportunities.

Citizenship and involvement

Citizenship is a helpful concept for exploring involvement because it is essentially concerned with people's participation as members of society. But there is no agreement about the meaning of citizenship. The political right has emphasised its obligations and responsibilities, particularly the obligation to find employment. The political left and centre have been concerned with citizenship as a basis for people's rights. They have highlighted the way that the citizenship of many groups, including women, black people and members of other ethnic groups, disabled and poor people, is qualified and their participation restricted. They draw distinctions between people's legal, political and social rights and show how restrictions on one limit the others (Lister, 1990).

In Britain postwar welfare state services were intended to compensate for broader inequalities and safeguard people's social rights as citizens. Not only did they largely fail to do this, but some welfare services created a separate 'service world' which increased people's isolation and further restricted their rights. Apart from blanket rejections of services for increasing state intervention and creating dependency, two strands can be detected in critiques of such a service culture.

The first places an emphasis on self-help, independence and people reclaiming responsibility for themselves. It questions the conversion of informal support into paid employment and harks back to the strengths of community and informal intervention, often associated with either a bygone age or non-Western societies.

The second strand is epitomised by the demands of disabled people and people with learning difficulties for equal rights, access and opportunities in the mainstream world: appropriate support rather than 'care' services to enable people's integration, and an effective say and involvement for people in such services as workers, users and other citizens. Traditional services are rejected as a 'social administration' response to people's needs, formulated by outside experts. 'Disability is a human rights issue requiring political action rather than a social problem requiring welfare provision' (Oliver. 1992).

It is important to be aware of this analysis because much of the recent discussion about the need for increased 'user-involvement' has been focused on such welfare services. People may be reluctant to get involved in services which actually isolate and inhibit them. The idea of involvement must be considered in context. It needs to be related to the social, economic and political institutions that affect it. The concept of citizenship helps us to do this by reminding us of the relationship between the individual and the state. This is often ignored or underplayed in discussions of participation, as if people only need to get together and work out what they want for it to be achieved. One activist in the disability movement emphasised the importance of recognising the central role of the state:

> **'It's not just a matter of people getting together as a group, or according to how strongly or weakly they put their case to the local or central state. The state is pro-active, not just reactive. There are barriers. If it's at the wrong time or the wrong context, it won't work. It's not just a matter of coming up with demands, but also to know how political structures operate to feed in your initiative with the best chance of succeeding. People need to learn how the state operates.**
>
> **Having more say and involvement aren't achievable unless you have some notion of the state. It is not a neutral arbiter. It has its own view of citizenship. It will try and push movements in ways which fit in with its own interests. If you don't understand the nature of the beast you are never going to address these issues. The state will try and subvert what you are doing and divide you.'**

But it is not just the state that excludes people. Many other institutions and organisations do too. The agencies and structures which seek to bring about change also often exclude people themselves. This has led disabled people to draw a distinction between organisations *of* and organisations *for* disabled people, to distinguish between those that they control and those controlled by another group.

The disability movement, like other new social movements, not only seeks the involvement of its *constituency*, but also the *large-scale* involvement of people within it. Its objective is people's participation, not pressure group politics. 'The only way forward is to fully involve disabled people in their own political movement' (Oliver and Zarb, 1989). Herman Ouseley made the same point about black people in the context of decentralisation:

> **'Decentralisation will only assume real meaning for them if they are fully involved in every aspect of its operation. If not then decentralisation will merely pass on some of the powers of the local State apparatus to known activists without changing the status quo . . . Any watered-down local arrangements will be regarded with scepticism.'** (Ouseley, 1985)

The same philosophy underpins this book. It is concerned with enabling people's broad-based involvement. Our view is that only by involving people in this way is it possible to develop services that are appropriate and accountable, neighbourhoods that meet their needs and structures that are democratic and accountable. Our concern is not only with challenging the oppressions and inequalities that people face, but also doing this in a way which fully involves them themselves. People's involvement is both the end and the means. The two cannot be separated.

Disagreements and difficulties

It's important to remember that current ideas about involving people are far from new. They have an unbroken history stretching back more than 20 years. They are a child of the 1960s. If the talk now is of consumer and community involvement, then it was of 'participation'. But such public participation had a poor track record. It may actually have increased rather than reduced many people's sense of alienation and disenchantment. High hopes were placed on it, but it was always ambiguous. It could be put to many negative uses, serving, for example, to sidetrack opposition, incorporate local people, give an appearance of action, create further delay, legitimate decisions that had already been made, set people against each other and provide a public relations gloss. We have seen instances of all of these.

In Britain public participation was most developed in land use planning where provisions for it were embodied in legislation. In 1972, one man, campaigning against redevelopment where he lived, wrote:

'Millfield benefited greatly from the termination of public participation in planning . . . In Millfield . . . specific issues connected with the planners' proposals were brought to a moderately successful conclusion (from the residents' point of view) only when the planners' rules were abandoned and the ordinary machinery of local councillor, MP, publicity, public discussion and so forth was utilised.' (Dennis, 1970)

This is an inheritance which participatory initiatives still have to live down. It also offers a warning. We shouldn't assume that widespread support for people's involvement means there is any consensus about it. We may not all mean the same. Different aims, interests and ideologies are involved. Overlapping rhetoric may disguise real differences. Many people are suspicious of an increased official interest in citizen involvement which seems to coincide with the run-down of the British welfare state and growing constraints on local government. What some see as initiatives to increase people's involvement, others may reject as an attack on it. For example, legislation in Britain to give council tenants a vote on the management of their housing was heralded as a way of increasing their choice. Subsequently it was widely condemned by tenants' organisations as a covert policy of privatisation. Giving parents the opportunity to vote for schools to opt out of local authority control was presented as a way of increasing parent power. But it has been criticised for placing more control in the hands of distant, less accountable bureaucrats.

It's also important to remember that there are different pressures for participation. These can come from agencies and services themselves, perhaps as a means of managing criticism and dealing with dissatisfaction, from people using services and their supporters, to seek redress and gain a say, and from other citizens – the 'community', as it's often called – who may be unhappy with both the others. Each of these is likely to have have different agendas and objectives.

Clarifying the issues

Citizen involvement may always be contentious because of its essentially political nature. But the ambiguities and disagreements that surround it also emphasise the importance of being clear what we mean by it. Clarification is a crucial first task if we are to make progress in involving people. Otherwise it is likely to mean all things to all people and satisfy nobody.

Approaches to involvement

Two key approaches to involving people can be identified – the *consumerist* and *democratic* approaches. Both may have their merits, but they should not be confused. They are very different. The emergence of consumerist thinking in health and welfare services has coincided with the expansion of commercial provision. Service users or clients are now conceived of as consumers or customers and issues reframed in terms of market preferences, consumer rights and product development, echoing the language and thinking of the market economy from which they have been borrowed. Consumerism starts from the idea of buying the goods and services we want instead of making collective provision for them. It places an emphasis on concepts of individual choice and competition. Two competing meanings underpin the idea of consumerism:

first, giving priority to the needs and wants of the 'consumer', and second, framing people as consumers and 'commodifying' their needs; that is to say, converting these needs into markets to be met by the creation of goods and services.

The democratic approach is about more than having a voice in services, however important that is. It's also concerned with how we are treated and regarded more generally and with having greater say and control over the whole of our lives. The idea of empowerment is central in the democratic approach. Its objectives are civil rights and equality of opportunity. Disabled people campaign for their right to access to buildings and amenities, to 'public' transport, to vote – often debarred by polling stations which are inaccessible to people in wheelchairs – and even the right to be born. People with learning difficulties struggle for the same reproductive rights and rights to their sexuality as other people.

If the consumerist approach is essentially service-led, beginning with the service providers' needs, not the consumers', the democratic one is *citizen*-led. It is concerned with people having the chance to speak directly for themselves. These two approaches to involvement have different origins and objectives. The politics of liberation don't necessarily sit comfortably with those of the market-place.

What involvement means

As well as being the subject of different philosophies and theories, citizen involvement has many facets of its own. It will help us make more sense of it if we start charting some of these.

When people talk about getting involved they most often mean helping out in some way. This may be a matter of taking part in an outing for older people, fundraising for a good cause, organising a street party, running a stall at a fête or looking after the children at a playgroup. This involvement essentially entails some kind of voluntary work. It is on this that debates about being a more 'active' citizen have mainly focused.

But such responsibility need not be and is usually not accompanied by any increase in the say or control that people have. It can sometimes serve as a first step which leads to some say, like the man we met who helped out at an after-school club in a family centre and was then invited to join the management committee, or a single parent who gave the teachers a hand at school and was then asked to stand as a parent governor. But the two certainly don't go hand in hand. Control and responsibility are two distinct elements of involvement. In our experience, responsibility without control tends to be unattractive and qualified, just as control without responsibility creates problems. As one woman said to us:

> **'What's the point? You don't get paid for it, although somebody else does for doing just the same thing. And when it comes down to it, what you say doesn't count for anything.'**

Self-help initiatives often bridge the gap. As, for example, Nancy Crewe and Irving Zola wrote in the context of disability:

> **'Self-help groups were slow to develop . . . but they have flourished and become a powerful source of mutual support, education and action among people affected by particular health concerns or disabilities . . . While learning and working together, disabled people can combine their power to influence social and political decisions that affect their lives.'**
> (Crewe and Zola, 1983)

Working together to help each other can lead people to work together for change.

In this book we will primarily be concerned with how people can gain a greater voice rather than exploring voluntary action.

Different areas for involvement

There are different spheres for such involvement. These include people's:

● involvement in their personal dealings with agencies and services
● involvement in running and managing agencies and services
● involvement in planning and developing new policies and services.

There are strong incentives for people to get involved in the services that they use. It's the natural starting point for most people's participation. We want to know what's happening to us, get the best treatment we can and sort things out if there is a problem. It may be a young woman in care who wants to buy her own sanitary towels instead of having them bulk bought, or the parents of a child with learning difficulties anxious for him to stay in mainstream education instead of being segregated in a special school.

Getting involved in the management of services is a logical next step for some people. They may not just want better treatment for themselves. Or they may decide this is the only way to ensure it. They may want to work with other people to improve the service more generally. This can be on a large or small scale. It may extend to having a say in budgets, admissions policy, day-to-day decision making and hiring and firing staff. It may, for example, be a carers' group getting control of the management of one respite care bed provided by a health authority or a large scale cooperative housing scheme which residents manage themselves.

Most services are set up by someone else, so it's not surprising if sometimes people don't so much want a say in existing services as the opportunity to develop something else. What is available just isn't what they want. They'd rather have access to open employment, for instance, than go to a sheltered workshop, even with a place on the management committee. This might mean trying to set up a self-help initiative, becoming involved in the planning process of other agencies, or seeking new legislation. They might want to run their own services. In association with local authorities, disabled people have established their own independent living centres. Some disabled people run their own self-operated care schemes. Groups of black parents have come together to set up their own schools.

The kind of involvement people have in their personal use of services may also fall into two categories, which for simplicity's sake may best be called *reactive* and *pro-active*. By reactive, we mean opportunities for involvement and redress when things have gone wrong, for example, complaints procedures, and by pro-active, where there is a continuing involvement that can prevent things going wrong in the first place, for instance, by having access to your own records, a right to be at meetings where you are under discussion and adequate information to negotiate the process in which you become involved.

The arenas for involvement are diverse, from campaigning for a street crossing to having a say in a decision to restrict your liberty. Different kinds of settings and services pose different issues for people's involvement. So do the variety of relationships we have with them. Do we have the same expectations of being involved in the doctor's surgery as in the local play service? What are the practicalities of gaining a say in street maintenance compared, for example, with ensuring access to rural footpaths? Our contact with a service may be one-off, sporadic, or continuous and long term. Each raises different questions. How can you make your views felt if your involvement is short lived? How easy is it to challenge a service if you feel permanently reliant on it?

Social services, for instance, include residential, domiciliary, fieldwork and day-care services. The service may be in your own home, an office or a centre you go to during the day for lunch and recreation. You may have asked for it or it may have come to you. Each has different connotations for people's involvement. It can demand a very different state of mind and set of skills to ensure an equal say in an essentially private, possibly intimate one-to-one relationship that has come past your front door, to those needed to get your opinions across effectively to staff in a lunch club. Yet both are about having a say in social services. And having that say is not just about being involved in a particular service but also determining whether it's *that* service you actually want. It is not simply a matter of setting up a residents' committee for people living in an old people's home, important though that might be, but making sure that they have a real choice in deciding whether they want to live there in the first place.

The involvement of different groups

There may also be differences between groups, for example, families with small children, people with learning difficulties and young people. While their demand for involvement may be the same, how it is best met need not be. We look specifically at the involvement of children in Chapter 4 when we discuss equal access and opportunities.

Different groups seem to have had varying degrees of success in their efforts to gain a voice. In social services, although it is still limited, most progress seems to have been made by disabled people and people with learning difficulties, much less by older people and families with children. Understanding why may offer us another clue to increasing citizen involvement.

Are older people inhibited by the low value placed upon them in our society and their own low expectations? Have organisations of disabled people benefited because people may be disabled irrespective of social or economic origin, giving them a very wide range of abilities, experience and talents to draw upon? How much has it helped people with learning difficulties that they aren't seen as a threat and that particular attention has been paid to giving them skills to participate which we *all* actually need?

The poor record for parents' and children's participation in social services seems to reflect the low priority given to the rights both of children and of parents suspected of abusing them. Services like social work raise an additional issue for citizen involvement because they can restrict people's rights as well as offering support and service provision. Patients may be compulsorily detained in psychiatric hospitals to protect themselves or others. Offenders are required to see a probation officer. Someone confused by Alzheimer's Disease may have control of their financial affairs withdrawn from them. The social worker denies access to a father who has sexually abused his child. All involve a restriction of rights and freedom.

Involvement in agencies intervening between citizens

In such cases where service intervention is not of people's own choosing and elements of regulation and social control are involved, issues of user-involvement and personal and civil rights clearly overlap. It is here, where citizen and state come into closest contact, that safeguards for people's rights and say are most likely to need legal force. As we shall see, where rights may be restricted, the idea of citizen involvement, far from being inappropriate or contradictory, as is sometimes suggested, is likely to be especially necessary. One measure of how important this may be is that while black people are generally *under-represented* as users of social services, they are *over-represented* on the receiving end of their restrictive provisions.

It's also a reminder that such agencies are not only concerned with providing goods and services. This is also a reason why a consumerist model of involvement doesn't always seem readily transferable from the market to the public domain. Social and other public services have a second role. As well as providing services, they intervene *between* citizens. This mediation takes place in two contexts. First is where there are different, perhaps competing, interests between people, for example, between social services users and carers, between marital partners or between neighbours as in the case of a local conciliation scheme. Second is where the rights of one citizen are either at risk or invalidated by another, for instance, between children and abusing parents and between other offenders and victims.

There are growing pressures for such intervention, particularly where inequalities and imbalances of power between citizens disadvantage certain groups, notably on the basis of age, race, class, gender, disability and sexuality. Here services are concerned with safeguarding people's rights and say in relation to each other. Now the relationship between citizens as well as that between citizen and state is drawn into the arena. Such agencies have a mediating role both in the relationship between state and citizen and in the relationships between citizens.

Citizen involvement is as important in such agencies as in those providing services. Otherwise their effect may be double-edged. Instead of sorting out the differences between different or opposing parties, they may become just another problem for them both or reinforce the position of the more powerful. If intervening agencies are to reflect the interests of vulnerable citizens and not just their own or those of the state, then these citizens must have a say in them.

Different routes to involvement

We may be offered a say in our neighbourhoods and services, it might be something that has to be struggled for, or both these approaches may be involved. It can come from outside an agency's own participatory structures as well as from within them. We may be involved directly or through representatives. We may only speak for ourselves or we may have been chosen to speak for others. Oppositional as well as more consensual forms of activity may be involved. Participation is ultimately about opportunities to negotiate competing interests and whichever approach we use to try and resolve it, conflict is bound to be present.

The work of self-help and community groups and rights organisations makes this difficult to forget. They also remind us that people's involvement is as likely to be a *collective* as an individual activity. We may get together to do something about our treatment as a group as well as taking individual action about a particular problem one of us faces. We may seek a say in our own case by banding together with others as well as by acting on our own. That's why organising, group work, campaigning and community development skills are recognised as having an important part to play in participatory initiatives.

Citizen involvement can take various forms, but there are also different routes to achieving it. Three are crucial. The first is changing ourselves, so that we are better equipped to participate and enable other people's participation. Second is developing more participatory processes and structures in agencies and organisations. Last is changing cultures and climates so that attitudes to particular groups are altered and people's involvement comes to be recognised as an essential and valued activity in the wider world.

Different people may feel more comfortable with different approaches. There's no doubt that it can be difficult and frustrating trying to change organisations. Infinite patience, a commitment to interminable meetings and a high threshold for boredom sometimes seem the essential qualifications. Some of us may feel most at home working with people. Others have the special skills required for campaigning for broader change and thrive on the public speaking, media attention and PR that go with it. The different priorities people attach to these approaches may depend most on their personal make-up. There may be different opinions about which is best. They are all likely to be necessary.

Arguments against involvement

Despite the new interest in citizen involvement, many arguments are still raised against it. These may sometimes seem like old chestnuts introduced only to resist change. But it's important to deal with them, whatever their origins, if only to be clearer about the issues.

Critics ask if people really want to get involved, especially if they are disadvantaged or in difficulties. Is it fair to burden them with it? A report on a family centre referred to a few mothers 'feeling overwhelmed by responsibilities of management or harassed to join in activities'. One local authority leader said:

'We should not put upon people what they do not want to deal with . . . Councillors are supposedly the ones with power. Do other people want to carry the can as well? Should we ask them to?'

Sometimes people may not want to get involved. We should recognise this. There must be a choice. But all the evidence from research we have carried out suggests that most people, rich or poor, want a greater say in their lives and services.

'I think the people who are in need should have more say. Maybe one day, we will be in need.'

Whether people want to get involved depends crucially on what it entails. There is no reason why it should be a burden. If it is, then agencies need to look at the kind of involvement they are offering, instead of using it as an argument to exclude people. Getting involved can be interesting and fun. For example, a voluntary project serving two council estates in Birmingham asked local people what services they'd like it to offer in future. As one tenant said, 'In the beginning it was hard work. When we got things sorted out it was enjoyable.' People who took part were sad when the consultation came to an end.

Then there's the argument that what people really want are decent services rather than having a say in them. After all, who wants to be involved in sewers or rubbish collection, and most families clearly prefer homes with gardens to the tower blocks that were foisted upon them. But how do we know what decent services are if people aren't involved? The paternalistic assumptions that underpin this idea help explain many people's loss of faith in public provision.

Doesn't it make more sense to have the home help when we want him or her, rather than when social services think we do? We may want to have our baby at home instead of routinely going to hospital. It's not only important to feel in control of services that intrude intimately into our lives. Community architects have shown how people welcome the chance to influence the layout of their homes, the fittings and materials used and if they are disabled, to make sure they are really accessible. Then there's the question of whether it is really possible to have the services we want *without* being involved. The track record of agencies and services which don't involve people suggests it may not be.

As with many reforms, there's a tendency to set an idealised model of the status quo against the worst case scenario for citizen involvement. Efficiency is set against democracy.

Involving people may be a good idea, we are told, but it's cumbersome and takes time. Yet existing procedures for policy development are themselves often inordinately long. It's one of the reasons many people find it difficult to maintain an interest in them. Frequently they also don't work very well. And what's the point of making decisions quickly if they are the wrong ones?

Citizen involvement, critics say, will also mean more costly services. It will raise false expectations. Many people won't be able to participate anyway. More and more, such arguments look like excuses for an unwillingness or inability to devolve power. Most rest on little evidence and so far insufficient attention has been paid to evaluating them properly. Hopefully some will become clearer during the course of this book. Yes, as we shall see, involving people has resource implications, but there is no reason why people who get involved can't adhere to budgets like anyone else. In our experience people are quite capable of setting their sights realistically, if they are kept fully in the picture. We have yet to encounter anyone who has been incapable of being involved in some way or other.

This emphasis on people's inability to participate in their own lives persists among many health and welfare managers and professionals. But denying people independence and a say actually reinforces the problem, because then their talents and abilities are obscured and inhibited. Members of groups of disabled people, people with learning difficulties and mental distress all describe a similar process:

'The initial objection to us taking part was that we hadn't got the skills. Then we got involved and spoke up and they said we were unrepresentative. We hadn't really got learning difficulties. We weren't typical of disabled people. Or they'd say someone put us up to it! They just couldn't believe we can speak for ourselves.'

The argument that people are unrepresentative is one of those most often raised against their involvement. Representation poses some real problems, which we shall be looking at later. But it can also serve as a convenient excuse for continuing to exclude people. In the past representation mainly meant speaking on someone else's behalf without too many questions being asked about your right to do so. Now when people are trying to speak for *themselves*, it has become a much more contentious issue. We have regularly seen user groups attacked by agencies as unrepresentative. But what are they saying – leave it to us? What accountability can *they* claim? What gives them the right to speak? As one woman involved in joint care planning said, 'It's double standards. How many of the *professionals* on the planning team are there with the agreement of their colleagues?'

The case for involvement

A strong case can be made for citizen involvement on both practical and philosophical grounds. There is now growing recognition that increased cost-effectiveness and greater public involvement in the planning and running of services and amenities are not incompatible, but can be complementary. Resources can be used more efficiently, needs identified and met better. It's not often possible to point to precise links between greater public involvement and improved provision. Such studies still have to be made. But people's experience confirms common-sense expectations. One woman representing her community association on a neighbourhood consultative group said:

'It is very effective as a representative from the Council comes and hears local people. We discuss the problems of the area and what needs to be done. You can hit at the Council straight away. They've got to do something if they say yes to us in front of all these people. You can get the police to do something that way as well. We wanted more police presence and we've got it since we asked.'

But having a say is also important in its own right. It shouldn't need any other justifications. It reflects the value an agency or organisation places upon people. It accords with our democratic ethos. People place a high premium on it. Listen to what they themselves have to say:

'It's very important for people to get a chance to speak for themselves, without people telling them what to say and what not to say.'

'I think it is very important that individual women are able to speak for themselves and describe their experiences. You don't know what a person is like and how they feel unless you listen to them.'

Do agencies really want it?

Citizen involvement faces agencies and their workers with a difficult question. Is it something they really want? There are undoubtedly gains and rewards. Some organisations already report the benefits it has brought, enabling them to provide more sensitive and popular services. But it's no easy option. It's also likely to make their lives more complicated and difficult, occasionally leaving them feeling bruised and battered. There will be tensions and conflicts. These may have been there before, but now they come to the surface and need to be addressed.

Citizen involvement raises many questions. It may mean empowering people to do things with which agencies and workers don't agree. Can they take that giant step from paternalism? What about issues of equity, resources and priorities? To whom are service users accountable? No one is saying it will be straightforward. But there's a difference between recognising that there are difficulties to be worked through and erecting them as barriers to progress. We have seen both at work. Which is it for you? Your answer may tell you whether citizen involvement is really what you want. One practitioner referred to 'the enormous range of excuses people make for not changing'.

It is also important for organisations to be clear why they want to involve people. Their reasons may sometimes be open to question. They may be trying to strengthen their hand against another authority, as councils have in Britain, seeking the aid of local people against central government. They may want to challenge the power of another agency, profession or level of management. Such intentions can have damaging effects. If that's why you want people's involvement, perhaps you had better look for other solutions.

The effects for agencies of taking on the challenge of citizen involvement are profound. They are likely to become very different organisations. This may be too much for many of them. It may not always be best to confront them with the implications! It also raises a related issue: where the responsibility for change lies. The director of one campaigning organisation wrote to us:

'In reality, people who want to participate may have to learn the skills to play the service agency game, but "professionalising" people (so they are able to do this) is not really the answer . . . I think it's very important to emphasise that the onus for change is mainly on the service providers.'

Citizen involvement is unlikely to work unless it is based on a recognition that human beings are subtle, complex and full of nuances. It's important to avoid facile stereotypes. Most of us no more see ourselves as service users neatly slotting into 'user-involvement' than as suitable candidates for services imposed upon us by others. The imagery of involvement tends to emphasise convivial interactions between people. It underplays the joys and anxieties, fears and prejudices that are actually involved. One of the problems with sixties-style participation was that it was often presented in rose-tinted terms, as if it were a matter of agreeable people getting together to sort things out. If only life were like that! The very idea of sitting round a table with strangers strikes terror in many hearts.

As we hope we have made clear, increasing people's say and involvement is not just a matter of getting embroiled in service provision and planning. Discussions have tended to focus on services and service users. But there is much more to it than that. Few of us want a say in policies and services for the sake of it. They are only important to us because they have a bearing on how we live. We want to be in control of what happens to us.

That's why we want a hand in them. We want to be able to live our lives, have equal and satisfying relationships and feel that we have a place in our community. We want a job. We want a home. We want to be treated with equality and respect. We want our human rights. We should never forget that this is the starting point for most people's involvement and try not think of it in narrow service terms. Now let's begin looking at it more closely in practice.

2

First Steps to Involvement: Information-Gathering and Consultation

Invitations to get involved in our neighbourhoods and services have multiplied. They are mostly concerned with gaining our knowledge and opinions. The two main approaches are **information-gathering and consultation**. 'Tell us your views', 'Your opinion counts', 'What do you think?' They echo other activities which have become a day-to-day part of our lives and cultures, from political opinion polls to air-time to express our views about television programmes. Information gathering is probably best seen as an extension of market research, trying to find out what we know and think, but consultation, as the dictionary tells us, is also concerned with getting our advice and counsel. Our situation, experience and attitudes are the focus of both. They may be directed at people using certain services, particular groups of people or the whole population. They can be on a large or small scale.

Information-gathering

Information gathering may be a matter of a voluntary organisation finding out what unemployed people feel about employment training, a social services department asking all the people in its area what they think of it or a council canvassing inhabitants to get an accurate picture of a city's

23

ethnic and cultural composition. The search for more community-orientated approaches in social and other services has
also resulted in a growing interest in local needs assessment
and community profiling.

Information-gathering largely means survey-making. The
agency's target may be a sample, that is to say a representative range of people, or a population, for example, everyone
who lives in a particular neighbourhood, owns a car or is a
member of the public library. These can be opinion surveys
with detailed structured questionnaires or short user-
satisfaction surveys. They are sometimes completed by people
themselves and then posted or collected, or alternatively
undertaken by an interviewer. Each is likely to elicit a different response rate. The aim may be to obtain *quantitative* or
qualitative information. With the latter the object is not to
measure people's attitudes or experience but to explore them.
Sometimes the two may be combined.

Information-gathering can serve many purposes. For example, a large-scale local authority survey, identifying the
number and proportion of people with chronic sicknesses and
disabilities living locally, was undertaken to fulfil a statutory
duty, as part of a comprehensive review of services and to give
people a chance to speak for themselves. When there were
plans to close the local branch of a supermarket chain, a
community group in which we were involved surveyed local
people, first to find out if they saw it as a problem and then,
when it became clear they did, to take their views to the
company concerned to try and persuade them to change their
mind.

Consultation

Consultation can be part of a highly formal process required
by law or informal meetings in someone's house involving
people from just one street. It may just be a matter of
responding to a request for our views and opinions, as
individuals or members of groups, or being elected or co-
opted to formal consultative structures. It may mean calls for

comment as part of a process of legislative change, following an official report, or in the development of a national policy – like the strategy for mental health services in Wales. It could be a local authority request for comment and questions in drawing up guidelines to ensure safe and secure built environments. Written or verbal evidence may be requested. Examples include an education authority asking children with special needs how they feel about their education and the prospect of integration into mainstream schools; a two day workshop giving disabled people and people with learning difficulties a chance to tell a social services department what kind of services they want; a large scale consultation, including consultation with children, in formulating childcare policies; and a social services 'users' day'.

While, as we have seen, there is a difference in emphasis and consultation may be more structured, it's not always easy to draw a line between information-gathering and consultation. It may not be helpful to try. Certainly consultation suggests a more interactive process where people can introduce their own ideas and move the discussion along as well as responding to the issues raised for them. Information gathering tends to be a more passive exercise – essentially answering other people's questions. We can have more of a hand in consultation.

'It was good. We had a chance to say what we wanted. They let us talk. I could ask my questions. It was only a small meeting. The people organising it there seemed to understand it might be difficult for us. They'd give us time to get our thoughts together. You didn't feel you had to get in quick or there was a right thing to say. We did most of the talking.'

Often what is offered is a package which includes elements of both, for example, meetings, surveys and exhibitions. This kind of combination may be helpful because information-gathering with its random surveys can make a representative trawl of opinion, while consultation is often dependent on whoever comes forward.

The importance of listening

The philosophy underpinning these two approaches to involvement seems to be one of opening up and improving communication between agencies and people. There's recognition of the importance of their perspective, the need to develop a dialogue and get feedback from them. They are part of new ideas expressed in terms like 'learning from the public', 'public service orientation' and 'getting closer to the consumer'. At their best they are an acknowledgement that agencies and services don't necessarily know what people want, that it is important to find out and that policy and provision can't just be based on professional or political opinions.

Listening to what people say must be a good idea. It makes it possible to match services more closely to what they want and offers a clear sign that they are valued. It helps agencies replace services which aren't appropriate, develop ones which are and make improvements according to expressed demand.

A wide range of issues can be quantified and explored through consultation and information-gathering. For example:

What do people think of existing arrangements or services?
What do they know about them?
What would they actually like?
Are their views changing?
Are there differences between different groups and different people?
Do people know how to get and use services?
Does everyone have equal access and treatment from them?
What do people think about proposed changes in policy, provision or services?
What changes would they like to see?

Consultation and information-gathering can help agencies:

change their role and services
determine priorities

● evaluate performance
● explore attitudes towards them
● improve their image.

We only have to remind ourselves of commercial slogans like 'the listening bank', 'a business inspired by its consumers', and 'it's you we answer to', to appreciate the importance invested in the last of these.

Turning to more imaginative methods

Over the years information-gathering and consultation have been characterised by a relatively narrow range of techniques, like surveys, meetings, consultative committees and invitations to send in comments. They don't have to be. There are other more imaginative approaches which are attracting increasing interest.

One alternative to surveys is discussion groups, where people have the chance to talk together in a more informal and less structured way. But even questionnaire surveys don't have to be rigid instruments which reduce us to monosyllabic respondents. Instead they can be based on flexible schedules that allow participants a say in what is discussed. We used a schedule like this in in-depth discussions we had with a wide range of groups about their needs, changes in social services and the relation between the two. It gave them the chance to take off in different directions and explore issues that particularly interested them, while still making it possible to consider and compare their different attitudes and experience.

Another model, borrowed from market research, is the *focus group*. Here a group of 10 to 12 people with a shared interest or experience are brought together for a discussion using a semi-structured schedule. The common concern could be dog food or living in a residential home. This technique offers organisations an effective check on customer views to monitor progress and modify their products and services.

One local government worker described an approach he was trying to develop:

**'There's continuous sampling. You have continuous systems
of consumer feedback. Start small, asking say, about housing
repairs or meals on wheels. People feel respected. You can
praise managers where praise is given. You use a reply paid
postcard. "I hope you enjoyed this meal. We are constantly
trying to improve this service. You could help us by filling in
this short questionnaire." Then there would be a six weekly
review at the social services management team meeting which
looked at the results. Send out questionnaires and give some
prizes to encourage people to reply. We have the technology.'**

Methods being added to the repertoire of consultation
include quality circles, quality action groups, search conferences and advisory groups and panels. Quality action groups,
which appear to have developed from quality circles, are
composed of stakeholders in a service. In a staffed house,
for example, this would include the residents, workers and
perhaps relatives or advocates of residents and neighbours.
The aim is to improve the effectiveness of the service for
people through a cycle of discussion, planning and action.

The idea of a search conference is to provide a forum for
people sharing a common concern over a particular issue, but
who approach it from different perspectives, for example, as a
user or provider of services, carer or manager. The goal is to
reach mutual understanding of the issue and to work towards
a shared view of the possible future. Search conferences do
not deny the differences between people, and allow them
opportunities they might not normally have to express and
share their viewpoints.

One of us was involved in a consumer advisory panel
recently set up by a national voluntary organisation. It was
elected by a newly created network of service users. They
could have a say in the organisation either by direct consultation or through the panel itself.

Listening carefully

Like most things, information seeking and consultation are
easy to do badly but difficult to do well. While they are the

two approaches for involving people most often attempted and where there is most experience, all too often the same old mistakes are made. An excellent idea may be a lost opportunity in practice. For example:

A service for people with learning difficulties plans to expand. Before doing so, workers feel it's important to find out what people think of it and where it should go. A consultation day is planned in two parts: the morning just for service users and the afternoon for carers and professionals as well.

Service users are given different coloured badges and divided into four groups as they arrive. These are led by outside professionals so that people can feel able to criticise the project if they want to and not be uncomfortable about it. The venue is pleasant and well furnished. First tea and coffee are served. The project leader introduces the day. She stands at the front on a small platform. She speaks very quietly. Some people can't hear her. All the group leaders have been given a long schedule of issues to be covered. One of the groups is run by a young man called Vijay. At the end, people leave talking animatedly. This is the only group where the report-back is given by a service user.

Another group is run by Jenny, a community nurse. She never actually asks people what they think of the project. Instead the discussion wanders. There are flipcharts. 'Is there anybody who will write on the paper or have I got to do it?' Susan immediately volunteers, although it's largely Jenny who decides what should be written and ignores the suggestions of another woman, Anna. Anna mentions that she goes to college and a group to 'speak up for yourself' and asks why they hadn't been given a copy of the schedule beforehand so they could look at it. Her frustration seems to grow as the group leader, who talks a lot herself, continually interrupts people to say we must move on to the next issue or the next person. At one point Anna asks, 'What work do you do? Do you like your work?' 'Oh yes, yes, that's a good point, but we're really here to get your views. I'd be happy to chat to you.' Anna quickly subsides, saying 'sorry'. 'No, no, don't say "sorry".' But Anna doesn't say any more.

How could it have been done differently? It would have helped if there had been a clear, simple agenda which people had an early chance to see. A lively introduction would have got the day off to a good start. Group work skills can't be taken for granted. It's important to be sure that group leaders actually have them. A conclusion which rounded things off and also allowed people themselves to pull things together, however briefly, would have kept the day on course. It could also have offered the opportunity for them to decide what, if anything, they wanted to do next.

It's not just a pity when consultation or information-gathering exercises go wrong. It's a much greater loss. It's likely to have an extremely adverse effect on people's attitudes towards them. 'What's the point of ever doing that again?' If they are to be tried, it's crucial they are done as effectively and skilfully as possible. If there are practical limits to what can be done, as there almost always will be, then these should be made clear, so people aren't just left thinking 'they couldn't be bothered'.

Trying to do it well

Start by being clear why you want to talk to people. The first questions to ask are, 'What do I want to know?', 'Why?' and 'Who from?'. Is this the only way of finding out? How does it fit in with the rest of the agency's operation?

There are some ways of making information-gathering and consultation more effective we'd like to highlight now, although others will emerge during the course of this book.

1. Make it a positive experience

There is no reason why giving your views should feel like a penance. The director of a major consultation project emphasised the importance of making it enjoyable:

'We try and make consultations with carers pleasant and practical occasions, with clear start and end times. There's someone to welcome you and let you know what is going on.

We provide a good lunch. We ask professionals taking part not to eat until carers have all had *their* choice. We don't want them to be assertive at their expense. Professionals don't speak in small group discussions. They have their chance to say something at the end.'

The local government worker we quoted earlier described how he had carried out group discussions when he was a commercial researcher. There are much wider lessons here:

'We paid them for coming and bussed them in. They were held in nice environments. Groups would be recruited by women using their lounges. We'd invite them to a discussion. If they wanted to they might be told about the outcome, although usually not. They'd get tea and biscuits and be treated like experts. We'd be extraordinarily careful about our sampling. If the client felt there was a particular ethnic angle, we'd have a particular ethnic group. Otherwise it would be a representative sample. They'd be tape recorded and the best agencies would do a transcript and content analysis. They'd do it now and you'd get a report next week.'

2. *Focus discussion*

If information- or advice-seeking are to be helpful, they must be specific. Don't ask people enormous questions. Either offer people a practical agenda or give them the chance to work one out themselves. Tailor the exercise to what you can actually do.

'We fix on particular issues so that it's focused and can be of use. We ask people about particular things they can relate to.'

But there's a tension between making discussion manageable and restricting it. One suggestion to give people more choice in land planning is for councils to present alternatives. But then the crucial choice is already made and people can only respond to the options on offer.

3.   *Take nothing for granted*

If you really want to find out what people think, then help
them set the agenda. After all, if agencies knew what line of
enquiry to pursue, they probably wouldn't need to ask people
their views in the first place. Pilot surveys and flexible initial
group discussions can help.

Whether you are seeking information or guidance, build as
few assumptions as possible into the questions you ask. When
one local authority decided to decentralise its services, as part
of its consultation it commissioned a large scale survey.
People were asked what they thought about neighbourhood
offices and where they would like to have them, but never
whether decentralisation was something they actually wanted
or if the building of costly neighbourhood offices was the way
they would want it to be done. Instead of asking people what
they think of proposed changes, try and find out what
changes *they* would like to see.

4.   *Individual and collective discussion*

Talk to people together and on their own. People say different
things in different settings. One researcher concluded that
people were more likely to offer the socially acceptable point
of view in public, while more private accounts emerged when
the threat of social judgement receded. We are also told that
people's opinions may be swayed in groups. We have found
that group discussions give people greater confidence to say
what they want, as well as opportunities to bounce their ideas
off others.

5.   *Link listening with help*

These exercises put agencies in touch with people they may
not otherwise reach. It's an opportunity that shouldn't be lost.
Anyone selected for detailed interview in the local authority
disability survey we described was offered a visit from a
welfare rights officer, asked if they knew about the council's
mutual exchange scheme and if not, whether they would like

to receive more information. 'People used it as a legitimate means of communication.'

When we made a survey about loneliness among older people, although all those we spoke to were already in touch with social services, about a quarter needed further help. We could follow this up with information, advice, and by contacting the appropriate agency or worker. We phoned the duty social worker about an elderly woman whose housing benefit had been cut, leaving her with £15 a week to live on. We explained to a man with cancer who was about to be evicted how to go about getting sheltered accommodation, which he then did.

6. *Working through people's personal agendas*

People have often said to us, 'Nobody has ever asked me what I think.' It's not surprising if they come to consultations preoccupied with their own personal agendas, wanting to sort out something that's happening to them, their child or their street. A public meeting or group discussion may not be the best place to do this, but it may be the only opportunity they have ever had. Consulting organisations sometimes seem irritated by this and try and move people on rapidly. 'I'm very sorry we're not here to discuss your particular problem.' We have also seen it used as a diversion to sidetrack a whole meeting. Instead we should recognise the importance of allowing people the chance to express their personal concerns, however briefly, so they can get past them, make the connections between them and wider issues and then ensure they are properly followed up afterwards.

7. *Keep people posted*

If you ask people their opinion, the least you can do is let them know what you find out. It's always interesting to learn what other people think, whether they feel the same as you and what worries they've got. It's easy to do, but doesn't often happen. When it doesn't, it's likely to fuel people's suspicions of tokenism and put them off the next time there's an invitation to get involved. When a large health survey was made where we live, the director said a report would be 'widely available in the district . . . in an eye-catching format that we hope will attract people's attention'. But we never saw a copy anywhere, not even in our health centre or child health clinic. Yet there are lots of ways of feeding information back to people, from displays in public places and items in the local media to newsletters and leaflets through the door.

8. *Don't exclude people*

Make sure you don't exclude people. Unless special provision is made, questionnaire surveys are likely to discriminate against people for whom English is a second language, while self-completion questionnaires can create real problems for people who can't read or are visually impaired. If the focus is a service or amenity, only talking to people who use it may bias or distort the answer you get. For example:

> **'They were consulting people about the park. They had a mobile exhibition van there with a young man from the council. When I asked him, he said they weren't going to replace the children's paddling pool. It costs a lot to maintain and dogs go in it which means it could be unhealthy. He said there wasn't much demand for things for children. But they've let the park go to ruin. There aren't the things for children any more. They haven't filled the paddling pool for two years. So fewer and fewer families bring their children there and there are more and more people bringing their dogs. Then they say there isn't the demand for the paddling pool!'**

Consulting some people can show the importance of consulting others.

> **'Recently we've set up a couple of posts to consult with parents. We closed down a hostel after consultation with people with learning difficulties and parents involved. We wanted people to have the chance to live in more ordinary homes. Then we got an unbelievable amount of reaction from**

other parents whose sons and daughters weren't living in the hostel but who had always assumed they would send them there. The task of the two workers will be to consult with other parents and provide high quality information about alternatives.'

9.   Accessing members of minority ethnic communities

An Asian woman health worker, complaining about a consultation scheme in her area, said:

'I only got to know about it by pressing. I've spoken to other Asian organisations who haven't heard about it. They've made no real attempt to inform or involve Asian organisations. There are no interpreters or translation services available today. I've approached the project about letting Asian people know and got no reply.'

When no Afro-Caribbean or Asian carers came to a series of consultation meetings about community care, a project worker was appointed to make contact with them.

'The most successful way of contacting people was by literally going out and speaking to them face to face. We've being going out talking to ministers and pastors. They're the ones who will say "Yes. OK. We will definitely bring that up in the notices at the services or at a meeting." Before when the leaflet was sent to a church or mosque, it was just forgotten about or put up on a wall somewhere. Some carers were quite rightly a bit suspicious. They'd ask me a lot about this project and where I'd worked before and if they were Afro-Caribbean, where my parents came from. That helped relax them and make them more comfortable. Then I'd go back and fill in the questionnaire.

One thing you need is to be aware of the cultures of the people you are talking to. Talking to Afro-Caribbean carers was easy for me as I am Afro-Caribbean and I know how they feel. With the Asian carers it's different as I am not Asian. It meant it was difficult for me to know what they really felt . . . What helped was that there was an interpreter who was Asian. Sometimes I would feel as though I wasn't there. They would just be chatting away to her. Because she could speak their language they were really relaxed. I think there is more pressure on carers from ethnic minorities. The person they are caring for could well be the only Asian person in a day centre.

Also there is a general lack of information about services. That's another thing they commented on. Also they felt that when they were going to find out about a service, the attitude was "you're not entitled to it". They felt white carers knew a lot more about what was available and had far more confidence and success in getting what they need. For the Asian carers, the biggest barrier is language. They get the attitude that "you haven't even bothered to learn the language".

A lot of the black carers have got the attitude themselves that the City Council doesn't want them to use the service. This goes back to their past experience of when they came here and were denied services, for example, they couldn't get a council home or a job and now they feel they won't get anything.

We really needed more time and a lot more things would come out of it. For example, a lot of things have been raised in the black carers' group that weren't said to me when I did the questionnaire. People have built up confidence in the group. One of the things we're going to bring out in the recommendations is that this kind of consultation should be included in mainstream funding and should have much longer. I'm sure if we had had a longer time to do it and could keep going back to talk to carers we could get a lot more information. You have to recognise that black people are here to stay. They're not going anywhere! So you have to take these issues seriously.'

10.   Reaching out to people

As this example emphasises it's important to go out to people instead of expecting them to come to you. Responses to consultation exercises and initiatives tend to be biased according to age, race, class and gender. Even the apparent randomness of sample surveys can be deceptive. We encountered a skewed pattern of refusals in one. Older people seemed to feel especially powerless and were particularly likely to exclude themselves. 'I've done these surveys before. It's silly, a waste of time.' These approaches can actually reinforce inequalities in access, giving a greater say to people who are conventionally more articulate or 'better educated'. Community development approaches offer a way of involving a wider range of people and helping them get together in their own groups to work out what they want.

When one local authority tried to consult women through public meetings, it discovered it was only reaching those who identified themselves as feminist. So contact was made with a wide range of women's organisations, including traditional civic groups, an Indian women's group, girls' and disabled women's groups, enabling a much broader spectrum of women to be heard. As a result, the women's officer concluded, 'it was not possible for management to hide behind the belief that it is only a small number of feminist or middle class women who want changes in the way council services operate' (Kettleborough, 1988).

Practical problems

Consultation and information-gathering both pose practical problems. They require considerable effort – much more than is often expected. It's one thing for managers to instruct workers to consult with people, quite another for staff to do it properly. Consultation and information-gathering are both labour intensive exercises and there are few short cuts. Organising a group discussion, an open day, or a public meeting can take weeks or even months of planning. Making contact, sending out invitations, organising publicity, making sure things run smoothly, all take time and trouble.

They also require expertise. If we want to make a survey, we need to know about sampling and designing a questionnaire. It's no use using untrained school students to undertake sensitive interviews with elderly people, like one team we

encountered. 'Seek specialist advice' is the first recommend-
ation of a workbook for social services practitioners planning
small scale enquiries (Addison, 1988). Even if an agency has a
research department, this kind of work may be new to it.
Agencies must either gain the skills themselves or buy them in
and that's expensive. Cost can be an important factor deciding organisations with limited resources against information-
gathering and consultation.

It may be hard work obtaining information, but that's only
the beginning of the story. These exercises generate an
enormous amount of data, much more than is often expected. It must then be pulled together. Sometimes the task is too
much and piles of flipcharts, questionnaires, transcripts and
notes are left to gather dust in cupboards or rushed reports
produced that do scant justice to all that people have said.

Broader issues

Consultation exercises expose people, perhaps for the first
time, to some of the realities of services and policies. They
hear about the lack of money, the long lead-in time for new
developments and the need to negotiate job changes with
trade unions. They begin to understand the way the system
works and the limits to change. It's an understanding we all
need, but it can also be disabling. Intentionally or otherwise,
the effect is often to inhibit people's expectations.

Even when it's collated, the information obtained is of little
use on its own. Ways must be found to incorporate it into an
agency's operation. A strategy should be worked out in
advance. We have been present at consultations where
participants are told, 'This is not just a talking shop. People
with influence to change things are here who will hear what
you've got to say', or, 'We will be passing on your views to
management'. That's not enough. Clearer questions need to
be asked if people's opinions aren't just to sit in someone's in-
tray. For example, what are the points of leverage in the
agency, whose responsibility is it, how can we get them to
listen and what action needs to be taken?

Nine key phases can be identified in effective information-gathering and consultation exercises. But they apply equally to all approaches to involve people. They are:

1. Identifying who you want to involve. Be clear who is the subject of the exercise. Are you only interested, as some agencies seem to be, in participants who you think will agree with you or make a 'positive' contribution? Are you looking for all people using your service, potential users or everybody with related needs?

2. Reaching them. Not everyone will come to you. How will you find them and how will you attract their interest? How will you ensure that women and minority groups are included? This requires outreach work to draw people in as well as invitations to get involved.

3. A published programme. A programme should be published and made readily available which includes the objectives, timescale and other key features of the participatory exercise.

4. Suitable forms to involve people. To ensure people's involvement it is essential to use forms and forums which are accessible, appropriate, familiar and effective. Traditional approaches like large public meetings and self-administered questionnaires are likely to leave out a lot of people.

5. Collating people's views. Collecting people's views and opinions is only the first step. If this information is to be put to use it must first be put together. Obtaining information takes time. Collating it is likely to take even more. It requires skill and effort and should be included in the timetable.

6. Feeding into the agency. Participatory initiatives have to be firmly located in the structure of the agency that undertakes them. Otherwise the information they generate is only likely to gather dust in a cupboard and add to people's strong sense of never being listened to. No participatory initiative should ever be undertaken until ways of incorporating its outcomes have been established.

7. Reporting back to people. When you have asked people for their help or involvement, it's important to let them know what is happening as a result of it. This is much more than a courtesy, although that's important in itself. It is a way of keeping people in touch with progress, developing trust and dialogue and keeping them informed about what part they have actually been able to play in bringing about change and improvement. Otherwise many people may not even be aware of it when agencies do listen to them. This demands the development of user-friendly information in suitable forms for all participants.

8. Initiating action. Participatory initiatives sometimes become almost an end in themselves. Because people are delighted that someone has actually listened to them – as very often no one ever listened to them before – this is seen as sufficient achievement in itself. But the real point of the exercise is whether the initiative leads to improvement and change. It should be judged by its *outcomes*. That's certainly how participants will see it. This is the crucial stage of the process, because it is the whole object of the exercise.

9. Monitoring the process. Unless participatory exercises are carefully monitored, it won't be clear how well they have worked, whether any particular phase of the operation has undermined it, or what might need to be changed. Consultation and information-gathering exercises still involve a lot of trial and error. Progress will only be made if there is a constant process of evaluating the particular approaches to involvement that are used and the way in which they are carried out. The findings of monitoring should be publicly available.

A participatory process

People's involvement should not only be the object of participatory initiatives and strategies. It should be built into them. Otherwise they are likely to share the same kind of deficiencies as policies and services which don't involve people – which they themselves are intended to overcome. Each of the phases we have identified is likely to benefit from people's involvement. They are likely to have some good ideas about how they can best be reached. They will know best what forms for involvement and what kind of information are most appropriate. Their judgement of the effectiveness of participatory exercises is a crucial one. Efforts to involve people should be based on a participatory process as well as have a participatory goal.

A checklist for information-gathering and consultation

It makes sense to ask people their views and advice, but it can clearly be difficult and demanding. This shouldn't put organisations and authorities off trying. But it does emphasise the importance of a coherent and systematic approach to consultation and information-gathering if we want to make the most of them. We can start with a simple checklist.

● Why do we want to do it?
● Who do we want to ask?
● What do we want to find out about?
● What's the best way of doing it?
● How do we want to use it?

Asking people what they want also raises much bigger questions which are less often discussed. It's equally important for agencies to take these into account when developing strategies for involvement. The rest of us certainly seem to when we're deciding whether to respond to their invitations to tell them what we think. They may lead us to a very different approach to citizen involvement. Let's see why.

3

From More Responsive Services to a Direct Say in Decision-Making

The limits of communication

The argument for information-gathering and consultation has been a simple one. People aren't being heard. Councils are unresponsive because they are out of touch. Welfare agencies are insulated from their clients. Boundaries have become barriers. 'Listening to the voice of the consumer' could overcome this. But is the key problem stopping us from having a say really one of communication? Is it just because they don't know what we want that the people running our services and neighbourhoods get things wrong? It seems doubtful.

First, social services and other agencies already have a vast amount of information about our views. Staff are in constant contact with service users and develop their own body of knowledge about them. Councillors hold surgeries, departments receive suggestions and complaints, records are kept and statistics collected. Yet how much of this information is actually used to plan and deliver services?

Second, when organisations try and find out more, the difficulties are not just technical. Yet the emphasis in 'getting closer to the consumer' has been. There's no shortage of expert advice. 'Instead of public meetings with a platform and audience, break up into small group discussions.' 'Try suggestion boxes.' 'User panels can be helpful although it's difficult to keep them together as people move on or lose interest.'

There's nothing wrong with this. We believe it's important to experiment and innovate too. But on its own, it doesn't seem to be enough. The politics of participation must be understood as well.

Fifteen years ago we were involved in a major public consultation as part of the development of our local district plan. Most of the methods now being advocated were employed: surveys, exhibitions, street meetings, small discussions, open forums, informal contacts, meetings with individuals and groups, newsletters, a telephone hotline and comment boxes.

However, in spite of posters and leafletting all over the area, most people didn't even know about the exercise and only a tiny proportion took part. It seemed to be undermined from the start by people's suspicion and distrust of the local authority.

'When they ask, they do the opposite. You always get the impression when they ask, they've already decided. They have a matter of fact attitude. They do what they want whatever we say.' (Beresford and Croft, 1978)

This isn't unusual. Efforts to set up local welfare advisory committees recommended by the Barclay Report on social work met with little response. The National Consumer Council found that 'the vast majority of people who were dissatisfied with local services did not do anything about their complaint' because they felt nothing would happen (National Consumer Council, 1982). Hundreds of patient surveys have been carried out since the Griffiths Report on National Health Service management recommended market research on consumer needs. But one enquiry showed that managers had rarely taken any action on them (Hyde-Price, 1986).

Feeding into their system

That's the basic problem with being canvassed or consulted. It's meant to give us access to organisations, but offers no way of making our views stick. Any inequality between agency and individual is duplicated in the relationship between consulter and consulted. Instead of overcoming our exclusion, they may confirm it. At the heart of these approaches to involvement lies an imbalance of power. When people don't respond, it's often blamed on apathy or inertia. Their comments tell a different story.

'What's the point of telling them they should have more houses for rent when you know they've got a council house sales policy?

You see these notices from consultative committees saying "we want your views", but they've got no power themselves.'

One development worker said:

'Consult the users, yes, he consults the users. He asks them what they want and then he goes and does what *he* wants. Consult the users? He doesn't even consult the staff. Oh, in one sense, he'll consult staff. He'll ask us and then later when we ask him why he's doing what he's doing, he says, "Well I consulted you".'

A member of a community group observed:

'If they like what you say then they tell everyone they consulted people. If they don't, it was only a few people and not representative. The say is always with them.'

Of course it's not always like this. It can be a positive experience. But agencies should expect to encounter scepticism and doubt. The difficulty is that this kind of involvement leaves the last word with the organisations initiating it. People feed into *their* system. They set the agenda, interpret the information and decide what to do with it. The dialogue that develops may be no more than *us* giving *them* our information and *them* telling *us* their decision.

Public service organisations are increasingly seeing market research and consultation as ways of improving their management. These techniques can help them get their priorities right and make less painful cuts. Many of the new methods being introduced, like quality circles, search conferences and focus groups, are management tools borrowed from business. But an agency's definition of how it can manage its services better may not be the same as that of its users. They may just be left feeling more closely controlled. Agencies say they want to learn from their users. But why should users of services regard it as a priority to teach them, especially if they themselves are tired, unsupported and overburdened? The interests of the two aren't necessarily the same.

The 'needs assessments' carried out by social services, for instance, raise concerns about people's privacy and civil rights. There is no indication of how local people or service users would have any control over the collection or use of the sensitive information sometimes involved. Fears have already been expressed about racist gossip becoming incorporated as fact. The health survey carried out in our inner city area focused attention on individual causes of ill-health to the exclusion of wider issues like low income, poor housing, environmental pollution and the high-profile advertising of health-damaging products.

A major supplier of commercial sheltered housing for retired people runs regular consumer panels for present and prospective customers. The stated aim is to improve their service, but at one we went to, people were asked to comment on their sales brochures, testimonial advertisements and promotional videos. 'What was your reaction to that?' 'Can you relate to it?' They are rewarded with a small supermarket voucher. One of the organisers said:

> **'Some of the sessions I have run have become quite emotional, especially when people were talking about maintenance charges and how they go up each year. Some people do worry about them going up and I think they are finding it difficult to manage. That does get rather emotional and I find I have to move quite quickly on.'**

Setting our agendas

Agencies and services also set the agenda in more subtle and complex ways. They condition our experience and expectations. It can be difficult to imagine what might be possible.

We speak from experience. After we had our first baby, we received a questionnaire asking for our comments on the hospital maternity service. We expressed our satisfaction. The only suggestion we had to make was that mothers should be able to go out into the garden. I (Suzy) hadn't been outside for a week. When we had our second baby at another hospital, we saw our experience in a different light. You could have your baby with you all the time and not just at feeding times defined by the staff. Visiting times were no longer restricted to fixed hours and a maximum of two visitors. You could breast-feed whenever you wanted, instead of being stopped when visitors were there. There were no more lectures from the sister before women left saying that she 'didn't want to see us back in the ward this time next year'.

A project worker wrote of one information-gathering exercise:

> **'In retrospect I have some disquiet about the way in which we framed our questions. Whilst users were free to disagree or to be critical, it was at least possible that, to some extent, they did not do this because they did not see how things might be different. It is very hard for anyone, at whatever age, to imaginatively "think on their feet" when presented with a series of questions about services.'**

Satisfaction surveys are tied to existing expectations and knowledge, instead of transcending them. Consultations frequently reflect our fears and prejudices instead of enabling us to think them through. The director of a project consulting with carers noted 'how little people ask for', in spite of the enormous strains and pains of caring. People who have never known someone with learning difficulties say they 'don't want them living in their street'.

From personal experience to agency data

The idea that agencies can find out what people think is deceptive. It suggests a well of objective data waiting to be tapped. It assumes that the methods they use are neutral and don't affect what people say. But our opinions aren't fixed. They change. They are also affected by the nature of our interactions. A variety of emotions and attitudes, from deference and fear of retribution to resignation and discretion, can condition our responses. As one person said:

> ' I don't like the day centre. But I'm hardly going to say it's no good, when they can use that to close it instead of providing something we want.'

Feminist discussions of research have highlighted these issues.

> 'The mythology of "hygienic" research with its accompanying mystification of the researcher and researched as objective instruments of data production [should] be replaced by the recognition that the personal involvement is more than dangerous bias – it is the condition under which people come to know each other and to admit others to their lives.'
> (Oakley, 1981)

The logic and technology of information gathering, however, pull us in the opposite direction, creating artificially hard data from the closed and multi-choice questions that are easiest to tabulate and computerise. The methods that come closest to avoiding these pitfalls, like group discussions and regular consultative panels, are the most time-consuming and most readily dismissed as unrepresentative.

Different approaches to citizen involvement

Information-gathering and consultation clearly have limitations as ways of involving people. They are:

> agency-orientated approaches
> controlled by the initiating agency
> primarily concerned with its needs.

This can:

> limit people's willingness to get involved
> qualify the development of their opinions
> inhibit the expression of their views.

It's wrong to expect too much from these two approaches to citizen involvement. But it's also a mistake to write them off. Participation is complex and subtle. Informal and consultative arrangements sometimes offer people more say in practice than more direct methods actually do. This is both their strength and weakness. They also have other incidental benefits. Even if agencies initially ignore them, they can help raise issues, spark off public debate, inform campaigns, provide publicity, and bring people together to decide what they want to do next.

An empowering approach to involvement

Let's look at them now in a broader context. There are a number of typologies of citizen involvement. Information-gathering and consultation come low down the scale on most of them. In one of the best known, Sherry Arnstein's 'ladder of citizen participation', consultation is categorised as a form of tokenism (Arnstein, 1969). Power is seen as central to an understanding of participation. Four important dimensions emerge in analysing involvement:

● who participates
● in what processes
● through what organisational forms
● with what degree of power. (Hallet, 1987)

Another helpful model has been developed in community education (O'Hagan, 1987). It distinguishes between services concerned with:

● efficiency
● enrichment
● empowerment.

With *efficiency,* the aim is to improve the effectiveness of the service itself. This is the role information-gathering and consultation mainly serve. 'Listen to what people say and you'll get leaner, more efficient services.'

Where the concern is *enrichment*, the desire is for people to get something out of the service too: new skills, competence and confidence.

Finally, where *empowerment* is the objective, people decide the agenda themselves. Agencies are unambiguously subordinate to their users rather than vice versa. No longer are we just concerned with the needs of the service but primarily with those of the people who may use it.

If this model comes closest to the **democratic** approach we introduced in Chapter 1, then information-gathering and consultation can be seen as much more closely tied to a **consumerist** approach.

The idea of empowerment is also linked with a third approach to citizen involvement which should be added to the first two:

1.   information-seeking/intelligence gathering
2.   consultation/advice-giving
3.   *direct say in decision-making.*

Here people are not just called upon for their views or advice, but they actually have a direct say in the decision-making process. Theirs may or may not be the only voice, but it is not subordinate to others. They have the power to influence what happens to them, to their neighbourhoods and to the services they use. This is the approach most clearly consistent with the democratic approach to involvement. If consumerist approaches to involvement are most often associated with information-seeking and consultation exercises, the democratic approach is most closely linked with people having a direct say. It allows people to speak for themselves. It is also inherently concerned with a process of *empowerment*.

It's empowerment to which we want to turn next. The distinction between empowerment and consumerism is central to an understanding of citizen involvement. The starting point of one is our rights and responsibilities as members of a society. The second is more narrowly concerned with us as individualised recipients of goods and services. Consumer protection seems to work least effectively for the most vulnerable consumers. The idea of empowerment is particularly linked with supporting those who are most disadvantaged and disempowered. We have already discussed some of the limitations of consumerist approaches to involvement. An empowering approach can overcome these. There are two objections to the idea which we must deal with first. One is about language, the other is political.

Empowerment is a rather grandiose word. Not surprisingly, some people feel uncomfortable with it. They wonder what it actually means. They point to its intellectual shortcomings. They describe how it has been devalued and misused. That's certainly true. Most recently we came across 'self-empowerment' used to mean something like pulling yourself up by your bootstraps! But we don't resolve the problem by ignoring the term. Instead we should define it. If we are concerned to increase people's say in their lives, services and society we must find language to discuss it. Unless we are clear what we mean by them, whatever words we use will be debased, like 'participation' in the past.

Here we use the term 'empower' to mean making it possible for people to exercise power and have more control over their lives. That means having a greater voice in institutions, agencies and situations which affect them. It also means being able to share power, or exercise power over someone else, as well as them exercising it over you. One objection that is raised to this is that you can't give people power. They can only take it. Nobody is going to give it away. Perhaps, but what this may really tell us is that it is more helpful to think in terms of helping or equipping people to take power than trying to give it to them.

Then there is the second objection to empowerment. The idea is often alarming to existing powerholders. Nobody wants to lose what they have. 'If they have more say in making decisions, then I'll have less.' This has been a major obstacle to more participatory policies and services. People are frightened they will lose control over their jobs, skills and responsibilities. But empowerment does not just mean taking power from one and giving it to another. It doesn't necessarily mean losing power. It is not a zero-sum; so that if I have more, then you must have less. It's also a mistake to think we automatically empower others by disempowering ourselves. Instead empowerment is concerned with changing the nature of the relationship between participants. This can have benefits for all. This is where it differs from consumerism, where any attempt to alter the balance of power between service provider and consumer often only emphasises the inherent antagonism between the two. As one social worker said:

> **'I've had to learn to work in a different way. I've learned to ask rather than tell. In one way it's easier to make decisions behind people's back – them not being at a case conference, say. But if you do it together, if it's you and them having to agree something together, it means something quite different – for both of you. They see you differently. They behave differently. Now I feel better doing it like that.'**

Two key components for effective involvement

That brings us to another distinction it is important to draw if people are to have an effective say in their lives and services. First they must have the personal resources and skills to participate, then the organisational and political access to do so. The two key components are :

 access
● support.

Support for people's involvement includes both **material** and **personal** support. We shall be looking at these in more detail shortly.

Efforts to empower people must both equip them for and give them access to a greater say. People need to be offered support and skills to take part, combined with suitable structures and opportunities for involvement. Unless both are present people may either lack the confidence, expectations or abilities to get involved, or be discouraged by the difficulties entailed. Focusing on one of these aspects of involvement to the exclusion of the other is unlikely to be helpful, yet this is what often happens. If doors remain closed, then all people can do is knock harder, whatever their personal qualities or abilities. Supporting people's involvement is not an alternative to addressing the inadequacies of institutions and organisations. We shouldn't only think of empowerment in terms of personal empowerment. It's not just because people lack skills, confidence or resources that agencies are often a problem. On the other hand, if people aren't supported to participate, then they won't be able to make full use of any opportunities that are provided. Only the most determined, experienced and confident people will then take part.

This is one reason why there is often such a difference between people's **formal** and **actual say**. It also helps explains biases in who takes part and how effective their involvement is. Unless people are equipped to participate, participatory initiatives are likely to mirror and *perpetuate* prevailing race, gender, class and other inequalities instead of challenging them. Whatever kind of involvement is entailed, from information-gathering to a direct say, it's important to be ready for it. Supporting and accessing people's participation are essential parts of the same process of empowerment. They reflect the **personal** and **political** aspects of citizen involvement.

Once when we raised this point, an activist expressed concern. She argued that people were quite capable of doing things anyway. 'They have lots of skills. Why all this talk of empowering them?' We don't intend to patronise people by implying they have limited abilities. Nor are we denying the validity of anyone's culture or experience and suggesting they need to learn someone else's. The issue goes much deeper.

Supporting people's involvement

Becoming involved can put people under severe pressure. They pluck up courage to speak at a meeting and are then utterly deflated when they aren't called. If they are, they may be so nervous they can barely speak or they ramble on in fright. The settings for people's involvement are often alien and intimidating: the council meeting room or an imposing office where people can lose sight of their own skills and feel they should be on their best behaviour. People feel anxious about procedures they don't understand, which have never been explained, but are reluctant to say anything in case it's their fault. They worry whether they can cope with all the meetings involved, feel guilty they are putting their children second but don't dare suggest it might be done differently. We have seen people reduced to tears and silence, their hands shaking, made to feel foolish or cowed into agreement. It has happened to us. For many, once is enough. Sometimes it's unintentional. Professionals and politicians just don't realise the effect they are having. On other occasions, it's because of their determination to stay in control.

Some of us face additional problems. This is particularly true for people using social services. Young people in care, disabled people, people with learning difficulties and mental distress are devalued and marginalised groups. Prevailing stereotypes are negative. Poverty cuts people off from activities which others take for granted. Increasing frailty erodes older people's self-confidence. Some services are themselves disabling. Institutional and residential provision narrows and inhibits people's expectations and experience. It socialises us into dependent roles and relationships. Segregated services isolate us from other people. The overall effect is to limit people's opportunities and choice and undermine their feelings about themselves and their abilities.

However, it would be a mistake to think that it's only people experiencing disadvantage and discrimination who have difficulties gaining a say. We have encountered retired professionals who had no idea how to negotiate the care system. We have heard from development workers about the difficulties they have had trying to get a say in *their* community. As one member of an organisation of disabled people said to us:

'Very few people have a perception of how they can influence what goes on in their lives, for example, the influence they can wield in local politics . . . The daily grind means they may not have the motivation or feel they can do anything. Most people are ill-prepared to participate.

Being involved is not the norm in our society. Few of us are active members of political parties, trades unions, or community organisations. As children we have little say in school. The pattern tends to be repeated in our workplace. Not only are our expectations of the agencies and services with which we come into contact likely to be low. We probably don't expect to have any say in them. They, on the other hand, have long experience in maintaining the status quo and absorbing or deflecting criticism. Very often it takes a crisis like a threat to their family, home, or well-being for people to try and get involved and only then do they discover what a struggle it can be.

Earlier we drew a distinction between material and personal support for people's involvement. There are two crucial aspects to supporting people's involvement:

● resources
● personal change.

They underpin four key components which enable people's involvement. These are:

● personal development
● practical skills
● practical support
 support for people to get together and work in groups.

People need resources to get involved, for example, childcare, transport, travelling expenses or respite care to go to a meeting or get together, and also training and information. We all need knowledge and skills if we are to have a say in our services and neighbourhoods. Finding out about a new service gives us a yardstick to judge the one we receive. We can learn how to budget or speak in public. Financial support, back-up services, training and information all have an important part to play in supporting people to participate and we shall be looking at them in more detail in the next chapter. But agencies trying to enhance people's participation emphasise another essential ingredient.

The importance of confidence-building

Enabling involvement is not just about equipping people with a set of techniques or facts, however valuable these might be. First we need to be in a position to use them. A more fundamental change from within is needed if they are to be effective. It begins with people's feelings about themselves and their abilities. If these aren't positive, progress may be slow. They may know what to do, but just not be able to do it.

The group worker with a single parents project said:

'We do a lot of training with single parent groups. Some of it centres around practical skills, for instance, how to plan a day or run a committee. But confidence-building I think is crucial. If there's a new group going I'll generally concentrate on this to start with. It's no good expecting a person to join a single parent group and make phone calls when (1) they don't have a phone at home; (2) they never use the phone; (3) they are afraid of the council officer on the end of the phone. The result is (4) – they don't come back to the group. Many people coming to single parent groups have been through very traumatic relationships and their self-confidence is at a very low ebb. It's crucial to build it up.

This means being careful in other ways too. I always use training cards in sessions that are written in large clear letters. Many people do not have very good reading and writing skills and being handed a card they can't read terrifies them. I also get people to work in pairs or threes and usually then one person will be able to read OK and can read for the group. I don't use words like "role play". It frightens people. I'll say "let's pretend so and so" and then I'll get up and play one of the parts and ask someone who seems confident to do it with me. Gradually I can encourage others to join and perhaps do things in small groups.'

A worker with a project helping people with learning difficulties to develop their skills said:

'I've come to feel more and more that people's problems are caused by their poor self-esteem and self-image. I've

developed work around that and made it a central part of our work. For example, in the one-to-one programme each person has, I get them to draw life lines and talk about themselves, their lives and achievements, not just the problems – to see themselves as unique and not just as someone with learning difficulties. We run self-esteem workshops, including group discussion, exercises and games over a weekend. We hold them further into longer training sessions when people have got to know each other and staff take part fully too.

Some people with learning difficulties appear to have far more "skills" than others. Often you realise in fact they haven't, but their self-esteem and confidence is so much better that they appear to. People can and do learn and develop far more when they feel good about themselves. It's the key to everything.'

Four crucial elements are repeatedly identified by user groups and others involved in participatory initiatives:

● self-confidence
● assertiveness
● self-esteem
● expectations.

When these are low, it's difficult for people to have choice and control in their lives. If people have been powerless, they are likely to be limited. One disabled man told us:

'People's self-image contracts to fit their experience. It's like institutionalisation. They adjust their expectations. You dislike yourself. You're a burden, ugly, devalued.

You recognise yourself as a source of anguish for others like your family.'

If people are to have a greater say, all four elements need to be increased. This is at the heart of the idea of *self-advocacy*.

'Self-advocacy means self-respect, respect by others, a new independence, assertiveness and courage. It involves seriousness, political purpose and an understanding of rights,

responsibilities and the democratic process.' (Williams and Shoultz, 1982)

The idea of self-advocacy was first developed among people with learning difficulties, although it has now spread much wider. It is concerned both with people having more control over their own lives, for example, living where they want to, managing their own budget, cooking their own food, going out when they like, and joining with others to pursue their interests more generally. It emphasises the links between the two. Both require confidence, self-esteem, and assertiveness. As we become more confident, we are better able to use and learn skills. As our social skills grow, we feel more confident. There is an overlap between the feelings and skills we need to live our daily lives and those we need to have a say in the neighbourhoods and services which affect them. It's another reminder that ultimately the purpose of gaining a greater say is to be able to live as we want to.

Gaining self-confidence

There are many ways of gaining the confidence and self-esteem we need in order to have a real say in our lives. They may come from friends and loved ones. Sometimes getting involved itself provides them, as we learn new skills and gain new status. We have heard from young people how the skills and state of mind they needed to survive being in care subsequently stood them in good stead when working to gain a greater say for other young people in care. But none of this can be relied on if everyone is to have an equal opportunity to participate. Many initiatives are now being undertaken specifically to support people's involvement.

For example, a day centre for people with mental health problems ran a series of six 'building up self-confidence' classes as well as introducing an assertiveness training course. A national campaign to enable older people to have more control over and increased expectations for their health, organised 'age well' days, supported self-help groups and produced accessible information. A project to rehouse single people with long experience of homelessness offered a package of personal, social and practical skills, so that people could 'take control of their lives and be able to live more independently'. The project's basic education worker stressed the importance of offering involvement in a way that's helpful:

'You've got to do it properly, otherwise it can be another experience of hassle and failure for people tagged as failures who may also be seeing themselves in that way.'

A social services department and health authority initiated a two day conference bringing together people with learning difficulties who were users of their services. This was part of a process of 'involving all adults in reviews and planning for their future lives'. A planning group made up of service users and an outside consultant met in advance to work out the overall structure of the event. When we met some of the participants at a follow-up meeting, they emphasised how positive and important it had been for them, meeting new people, sharing their experience, developing discussion. One of the workers commented:

'Their satisfaction with things like jobs has gone down since the conference. It's a good thing. People's expectations have risen.'

A young woman member of a multi-racial youth club said:

'When someone first comes into the running committee, they are offered a lot of support as a lot of people don't know what they're taking on at first. You don't know what to expect and it's more difficult than you think. If you don't help build up their confidence, they don't stay on it very long.'

Members of an an older women's project said:

'It's very important for us that this is an all women's group, dealing with women's issues. It's given us the chance to assert ourselves. Here we can fight together for women's things.'

'For me this has been the group that has broken through the formal rituals and conventions of organisations. In what it's done, it's given women confidence. I've seen women get up at the Pensioners' Association and speak extremely competently. Five years ago they wouldn't have been able to do that.'

A self-help group of people with AIDS reiterated the relationship between people being able to take control of their lives and services.

'People are encouraged to be involved all the time. The gain of this way of working is that it gives people confidence. We are in the business of re-empowering people after they are diagnosed as having AIDS. We are giving them back control over their lives.'

There's a tendency to highlight the importance of self-advocacy for groups like disabled people, and people with learning difficulties and mental distress. But it's something *everyone* needs. We can all learn from the progress they have made. The strength of self-advocacy is that it starts with people's ordinary day-to-day lives, experience and involvement. Its vulnerability is that it may stop there. As we gain in confidence and skills, we may be better able to deal with unsympathetic agencies and services which exclude people. But this should never be made the excuse for leaving them untouched. In the next chapter we will begin to look at ways in which they can change to involve and empower people.

4

Key Components for Effective Involvement

We have seen some of the personal implications of involvement and empowerment. Now we come to the implications for organisations and services. How can they provide opportunities and access for people to have a say? We want to look at eight elements that go towards making this possible. These are:

- resources
- information
- training
- research and evaluation
- equal access and opportunities
- forums and structures for involvement
- language
- advocacy.

But first a word of warning. Involving people is not just a matter of neutral techniques, but a *political* activity. Certainly there are helpful tools to use. For example, getting people together around a model to work out how they would like to plan their neighbourhood can overcome inhibitions and open up discussion. But if the politics of the situation also aren't made clear to them, for example, the powerful and competing agendas of developers and cash restraints of local authorities, then it will almost certainly be a futile and disillusioning experience. Nor is involving people just a set of procedures. It is a *process* of both personal and political change. If we

60

conceive it in mechanistic terms, we are likely to be disappointed.

It's important to remember this when trying to identify factors which encourage people's involvement. Issues of power and politics will always muddy the water. There's no simple and certain way of empowering people. But it's not a mystery either. The elements we describe shouldn't be seen as a recipe guaranteeing people a say in organisations and services. But existing participatory initiatives suggest they go a long way towards making it possible. Our list isn't exhaustive. Others may be different. Additional constituents will also emerge elsewhere in the book. There is no one right way of involving people. Many variables affect it. But whatever approach to involvement agencies adopt, information-gathering, consultation or direct say, these components are likely to be helpful.

Resources

Involving people does not necessarily mean that things will cost more. The argument that they will because people always want more does not hold. In our experience, given the chance, most people are quite capable of understanding economic realities. Involving people makes it possible to match resources more closely to need. It shouldn't be seen as a way of saving money. Sometimes more may be needed. But much can be done by reallocating what there is.

Citizen involvement, however, like any other policy, has its own resource implications. It would be a mistake to forget them. It can't be done well on the cheap. All the elements we discuss in this chapter require resources, both human and material. Citizen involvement demands time, space, skill and support, all of which cost money. But this should also be put in context. *Excluding* people's involvement has its own costs because it results in inappropriate and wasteful policies and services. The savings that involving people would make on these are more than likely to pay for it. As one manager told us: 'User-involvement may take more time at the beginning of the process, but less at implementation and it results in a better service.'

The range of resources required to ensure effective public involvement is wide. It includes places to meet, publicity, secretarial and administrative support, transport and travelling expenses, information and training. Parents need childcare in the form of a crêche or allowance. Carers need support so they can leave the people they care for. Independent consultants and advisers are likely to be needed to offer people skills and support. User groups need to be resourced if they are to be effective. User groups make a strong case for participants to be paid for their work and skills. One residential mental health project we encountered, for instance, paid residents to sit on its management committee in recognition of the contribution they made.

Take, for example, the claimants' commission one of us was involved in, set up to give consumers of social security a voice.

'All our expenses were paid in advance. If you haven't much money, it's no use being able to put in for it afterwards. It was made clear from the beginning that that's how it would be. You never had to be out of pocket. You didn't have to worry about things like would you be embarrassed or would the children be OK. It was all taken care of. We could go out and have a decent meal together, a real treat. If people were disabled, the secretary would order a taxi.

We had a well-furnished office with our own administrative help, all the resources we needed: photocopying, access to printing, postage and telephone. We had money to pay someone to come in and help us learn to work together. There was money for people to visit other projects and see how they did things.

We were all poor. Money was important. Once people got to know each other and got more confidence, it made it more likely they'd enjoy it and want to keep coming. Instead of being devalued as claimants, as you usually are, you were treated with real respect for the experience that gave you. It made you feel valued.'

Such a situation is far from usual. As a local planning officer in the health service said:

'It's done as part of everybody's job. The odd hiring of a room, printing of a leaflet you can slip in here and there. The finance officer is tolerant of our vast number of sandwich lunches! I think it would be better done if properly resourced. You can't be explicit. It takes a lot of time. Say, if you've got a large number of relatively senior officers taking part facilitating a discussion of ten carers, then they may feel we shouldn't be spending all these resources just on this. You can't win. If you make clear the resource implications, then they can say, "Well it's not necessary to do that. That's just trimming." If you tell people the cost implications, it puts them off. If you don't and try and do it on the quiet, then you can never do it properly as you would want to. It's all hole in the corner, but at least you may be left alone to do it. If it's under the counter, it's insecure. What about the argument that they'll save money which is wasted if they keep doing it the way they do now? They've got to change their priorities.'

This kind of approach is likely to lead to failure. It's too much to expect workers to involve people in addition to all their existing responsibilities and without additional resources. Involving people requires skills and resources. The first step is for organisations and authorities to recognise this and budget accordingly. Space and time must be made for new participatory approaches.

Information

Without information we can't make rational choices. Without it we cannot give our informed consent. We need information to know:

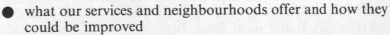

- what our services and neighbourhoods offer and how they could be improved
- how agencies and organisations work and how we can gain a say in them
- what is in our own best interests.

It's important to *establish the facts*. People can't easily make a good assessment if they aren't sure exactly what they are talking about. If we are talking about a service, we should start with what it's supposed to do, where it is, who it's for and so on. We need to know what a particular service entails, what new kinds of services have been developed, what else might be possible, what other ways of meeting needs there might be and how things are done differently elsewhere. We need information to increase our expectations and understanding.

Commenting on a health service study, a researcher told us:

'People were asked if their GP had given them a choice of consultant. Most said not. They were then asked if they would have liked a choice. Most again said not. Some people have taken that to mean that people don't want a choice. It is so daunting if people ask you a question like that. If the GP gave us more information about the skills of specialists and the various lengths of waiting lists, then perhaps we could make a judgement.

It's important that information is provided over a long time. It should be a cumulative process of gathering information, from health being discussed at schools, so that you are acclimatised to this approach and can make informed choices when it comes to it. Doctors should also be better able and more ready to communicate information to you.'

There may not yet be enough information about how to get involved. But a vast amount is produced about amenities and services. All the signs are that most of it makes little impact on people. That's hardly surprising when the prevailing images are of agency noticeboards and windows covered with dog-eared and outdated information, warning, advising or telling people what to do. Piles of leaflets pushed through our doors or stacked in racks remain unread. When, for example, we talked to people in one area about social services, we found most knew little or nothing about them, sometimes confusing them with social security.

If information is intended as part of a process of involvement and empowerment, some crucial questions must first be asked. They face user and community groups no less than large statutory organisations.

Who are we trying to reach?
Whose language are we using?
What information do people need?
When will they want it?
Where can it be provided most helpfully?
What forms will be most effective?
What support will people need to make the best use of it?

It's important for agencies to ask people instead of assuming they know the answers. We don't yet know what does and doesn't work. Great reliance is still placed on posters and leaflets. Yet most people seem to prefer word of mouth and people they know, like family and friends. Overloading people with large amounts of information is unlikely to be any more help than giving them none.

People should be involved in developing and evaluating information and given support to produce their own, like the tenants' association representatives who identified ways of improving information to involve tenants in housing improvements and the parents who with staff produced a new booklet about an intermediate treatment project for young people run by a large national children's charity, so other parents wouldn't be put off by the organisation's 'orphan image'. They also got agreement for parents, young people and staff to write the annual report together. The government department involved was 'a bit startled when it arrived'!

Research suggests that to be effective, information should:

be of immediate relevance; clear, attractive and brief
be appropriate to people's abilities, experience, knowledge, language and culture
take into account the particular needs of:
    members of minority ethnic communities
    people with limited mobility
    people with sensory disabilities
    people with limited literacy skills

● link verbal and written information
● be available from clear contact points
● offer the chance to get to know the information-giver, to develop trust and confidence.

A lack of information should not be used as an argument for denying people involvement. They can find out. We all have our own knowledge. We can become our own experts, like members of this community group concerned with land use issues:

> 'We'd find things out quickly by learning where to look, like the Estates Times or Company House. We networked with other groups. There were sympathetic officers who'd tell us things. The Council thought they were the experts, but we were telling them.'

The mother of a disabled child told us:

> 'You get told all the time she's going to die at two, then five, now eleven. It's your expectations against the professionals. They say children like these don't feel pain. That's what they said. You are actually devalued. Your judgements and ideas are set against theirs.'

A group of users of psychiatric services with other local health organisations produced a leaflet about the drugs people were prescribed and their possible side effects:

> 'First we circulated it to everyone we could in the wards. Then we got it printed and we got agreement to have it in doctors' surgeries and in the local chemists', so that each time when you get your pills the information's wrapped round the container.'

It took nine months to get official approval for the contents of the leaflet. It's important to remember that information is not neutral. Major tranquillizers are a good example. At a meeting where a researcher referred to his finding that many people valued this treatment, a former recipient said:

'People aren't given clear information on the options available, whether the medication actually will prevent relapse or what the side effects are. You aren't in a position to make a judgement without knowing what the full pros and cons are.'

But some professionals disagree with user groups about these drugs. The information they give may not be the same. One disability activist argued the importance of challenging the neutrality of *expert* and *official* information:

'The rehabilitation of people with spinal cord injuries is very physicalist – training people to get up, wash, walk in callipers if they can. There are other ways of doing these things, but these may not be presented by the rehabilitator to the person being rehabilitated.'

Because it can change our minds, information may be very contentious.

Training

Citizen involvement demands a new set of skills, ideas and values. *Everyone*, policy-makers, managers, practitioners, and direct and indirect service users, needs training, if people are to have more say. It should be built into professional courses. It should be part of our education at school. Trying to involve people without it is a recipe for failure, but that's what often happens. How can someone whose only previous experience is managing their personal finances be expected to control a large budget, without training or support? One member of the management committee of a community nursery who had no idea how to involve other parents, ended up saying, 'We should tell them to pull their socks up and get involved.'

Assumptions that people can't participate often ignore the contribution training can make. But making people's involvement conditional on training can also be discriminatory. The mostly black parents involved in an under-fives centre were denied a say in staff appointments because the local authority had so far failed to send any of them on the equal opportunities training it required. A man with learning difficulties was told he couldn't take part in a local planning and coordinating group because:

> **'Consumers had to have training before they could participate. But there was never any suggestion that the professionals on it needed it too!'**

When we talk about training for participation though, we should say that we don't mean passive instruction tied to books, desks and lecturers. Existing initiatives emphasise the importance of a more open and participatory model of training. When we asked people in participatory projects what skills they had needed to get involved, they referred to both personal and technical skills, like having the confidence to go to meetings and being able to make their points. They said they had mainly gained them from experience and by learning from each other. There's an important lesson here for training. People seem to learn best experientially and together. One example we came across was a service users' committee of people with learning difficulties who used video to improve the way they worked together. Another was a group of tenants hoping to move from inadequate housing to a new housing cooperative:

> **'At one session they divided us into groups of three. We practised being a spokesperson, chairperson and minute-taking and then changed round. That worked quite well. It did seem to make people talk more. But it wasn't quite long enough for people to overcome their embarrassment. People needed more of this and more practice as they were afraid to speak up at meetings . . . The women who did the training sessions were lovely people. You could sit and debate, argue and discuss. They put you round the table and left you to discuss a problem and then came back.'**

Let's now look at some other key training issues emerging from existing participatory initiatives.

People's two-way involvement in training

People who use services shouldn't just be seen as candidates for training. They can also provide it. Their unique perspective and experience offer valuable insights. They now contribute to professional training courses and conferences. National organisations of people with mental distress have provided their own training for user trainers. User groups run their own courses for agencies. For example, one of us was involved in a half-day workshop organised by a user group for staff of a large voluntary organisation, to explore user involvement and develop concrete proposals for working together. To prevent this being voyeuristic or patronising, it is important that people are treated like other speakers and trainers, paid and given the chance to offer their own analyses and solutions, instead of just being expected to talk about their personal problems.

Training and access to resources

Should access to resources be made conditional on training? We can see some of the problems if it is from what this tenant of a housing cooperative told us:

> **'Through all the twelve training sessions no one could be sure they would get a house. I think most people felt they were only attending anyway to get a house. I think people were inhibited at the training sessions because they felt if they said the wrong thing they wouldn't get one. People arrived half an hour, an hour early for fear of being seen as late arrivals. My husband was suffering from anxiety and depression at the time and he had to leave the first meeting halfway through! He asked if that would affect our chances. I'd have told people *before* the sessions, "Yes, you will have a house", even if you didn't know exactly where it would be.'**

We spoke to both workers and tenants involved in this scheme. One of the interesting issues that emerged was that workers had not realised that this was a problem and when we spoke to them it became clear that tenants had not felt able to feed back to them their worries.

Equal access to training resources

One training officer emphasised the importance of offering service users as well as staff access to agency training resources and budgets.

> 'They should be able to use them too. Practical problems quickly arise. For example, staff meals are paid for, but disabled people were expected to pay for themselves. I had to sort out about meals and travelling expenses. We've got to rethink who and what training's for.'

Joint training

Training people to work in services without their users being present is like Hamlet without the Prince. It cuts off a key perspective from the discussion and reinforces the gulf between people and professionals. Bringing service workers, users and indirect users together in training begins to break down some of the barriers. It offers invaluable opportunities to develop dialogue and exchange on more neutral ground. Take this social services initiative.

> 'We organised the first joint piece of training around normal-isation. The department identified a day centre which it knew wasn't functioning well – rapid staff turnover and underused. It was advertised for users and workers. All the staff from the unit came, except only two. Drivers and cleaners came and about 12 or 13 users. Some users came out of curiosity, some because they were angry. It takes three hours. It was asking workers to change. This was before there was a users' committee. Then we offered an Open University course – a

collaborative approach to working with disabled people, for both groups. Twenty-four wanted to do it – five sessions at five-weekly intervals. Staff were not on duty. They had to struggle to see disabled people as people and vice versa of workers. I think it shocked most social workers.'

Involving people in the development of training

Workers realised that training for new tenants in a self-managed housing scheme relied a lot on the printed word, so they also read out and explained what was going on. Members of a neighbourhood forum set up as part of decentralisation found their five training sessions 'too much like being at school', so instead a brief and simple written pack in eight languages was being produced. Perhaps the secret of appropriate training is to involve people in developing it. We sat in on a session at an adult education college where a group of people with learning difficulties were testing a draft version of a new Open University course for students with learning difficulties. An anthology which formed the centre piece of another course had an editorial advisory group made up of people with learning difficulties.

There is increasing talk about 'user-involvement', but it's a mistake to see people as a separate group of service users. This is more likely to be a statement of their exclusion from other opportunities than the identity they attach to themselves. Training has an important part to play in challenging people's marginalisation as service users by accessing them to employment. One Scottish social work department set up a social work trainee scheme as a response to the low level of applications for qualified social worker jobs from disabled people. One of the trainees taken on under the scheme said:

'It encourages disabled people who otherwise might not apply or who might find it difficult to persuade colleges and universities to take them on . . . [Being disabled] is a positive advantage. With clients there is no doubt that the first reaction is often one of shock and surprise. They see a little man in a wheelchair who is supposed to try to deal with their

problems. Yet that first look often breaks the ice and they can discuss things very much more easily with me.' (Hunter, 1990)

Research and evaluation

Research is an important dimension of any policy or practice. It's especially important in one as complex and contentious as citizen involvement.

Carrying out our own research

So far, research in this field has mainly meant asking people their views of services. It's important for people to be able to undertake their *own* evaluation of services, based on their own criteria, as well as feeding into those of agencies. Community organisations have long made such studies of housing and amenities. But people using services are now beginning to get the same chance.

For example, a local health authority and social services department commissioned an organisation of people with learning difficulties to carry out an evaluation of two group homes and local day services as part of its hospital closure policy. The two members of the organisation who carried out the research as consultants were both users of services and experienced in self-advocacy and as trainers. They had the help of a supporter, whose role was to assist but not to initiate and a researcher who was available to offer expert advice on research issues and:

**'comment on our work. We felt this was particularly impor-
tant because this type of evaluation had not been attempted
before.'**

The result was a report which led to change in the services and the publication of a book to help other groups carry out similar evaluations (Whittaker, Gardner and Kershaw, 1991).

Another initiative we have seen is a 'consumer' evaluation of a community mental health project for young people. This was based on a residential exercise and involved group sessions, using techniques like brain-storming and discussion; individual interviews, and art and drama sessions, to give people the chance to participate non-verbally. Later a follow-up meeting was held where participants could comment on an initial draft and a report was published which allowed participants' comments and illustrations to speak for themselves.

Researching citizen involvement

We need more information about citizen involvement. Participatory projects haven't been systematically studied. What knowledge there is, isn't widely accessible. Research is required to improve our understanding and evaluate new initiatives. It is crucial that efforts to involve people are carefully monitored and widely reported, otherwise much work will be wasted and progress will be slow. Some schemes and techniques have received publicity and support without any evidence that they actually work. It's easy to see why. People are desperate for help and some organisations are quite happy to encourage approaches which offer an appearance of involvement but leave them secure and unchanged.

Citizen involvement demands a particular kind of research consistent with its own participatory goals. It's not enough to rely on conventional professional perspectives. Evaluation should include participants' own assessment of initiatives to involve them. Their perceptions of participation may be very different to those of professionals. Only they can know what it feels like, what they want from it and how it can best be improved to fit their needs.

Experience so far suggests some initial guidelines for such evaluation. It should:

● be linked to participatory initiatives from the start instead of being undertaken retrospectively as is now often the case;
● be based on an action-research model where there is a continuing process of research informing change; and
● rest on a set of clear criteria, developed for assessing participatory initiatives, including exploration of partic-

ipants' views, equal opportunities policy, participatory structures, conditions of involvement, rights and outcomes.

People should be involved in the construction of research and supported to undertake their own. For instance, in a research project on an under-fives day centre, two parents were invited to attend monthly planning meetings and a representative group of parents were involved in interviewing other parents as well as keeping diaries about their contact with the centre and how well it reflected expressed ideas of partnership and participation.

It's important that research reflects the interests, priorities and values of participants, not just of policy-makers and researchers. What issues and information concern *them*? Research by disabled people has challenged prevailing definitions of handicap and disability, One researcher involved in the disability movement concluded that 'most social research . . . has contributed to the oppression of disabled people' because it ignored this (Oliver, 1987). As a member of a self-advocacy group campaigning for better mental health services said:

'We should think of research as *re-search;* to think again about what we have been taught . . . Unless recipients of services are part of the research, then you disadvocate them.'

A growing catalogue of participatory research reflects this, from the researcher supporting an oppressed pastoral community in Tanzania to express its voice, to work the two of us did to enable service users and other local people to offer their views of a social services department's efforts to involve them. It points to a changed role for researchers, collaborating with people to produce their own accounts and analysis.

Equal access and opportunities

Unless people have access to services it makes little sense talking about their right to a say in them. Access to services is notoriously unequal. Women make much less use of leisure and recreational amenities than men; members of minority ethnic communities are under-represented among users of care services, and 'public' transport excludes many disabled people.

Equally people may gain little advantage from having a say in services if the only reason they have for using them is that they are cut off from other activities and opportunities. What compensation is it for a person with learning difficulties to be 'involved' in a segregated workshop, when what they want is a job in open employment? Why should a young black woman denied access to ordinary housing take part in residents' meetings in the hostel she's offered instead?

It's important that we make this distinction and that people aren't just offered involvement in services as an alternative to the mainstream rights and opportunities to which they are entitled. Similarly, provisions for involving service users should reflect an effective equal opportunities policy. They aren't a substitute for it. Citizen involvement implies equal access and opportunities in three overlapping spheres:

mainstream life
support services
arrangements for involvement.

Moves to decentralise services have highlighted the importance of geographic access. But this is really only the beginning. Four other kinds of access must be addressed to challenge discrimination.

physical access to buildings – ensuring an accessible environment to disabled people and others with limited mobility
language – enabling everyone to communicate on equal terms
psychological access – the unspoken messages and the feelings we have; the sights, sounds, cultural and spatial cues, that tell us whether we are welcome and want to be somewhere
time – services available at times to meet the needs of all users.

Interpreting highlights the importance and some of the complexities of access. This is what some interpreters for hearing impaired people said to us at a conference looking at services for people with a sensory disability.

'You can't do it on the cheap. They had a service user on the planning committee but they didn't listen to her suggestions. They didn't listen to the issues interpreters raised in advance. It may make sense for them to lump together people with visual and hearing disabilities. Workers are organised for both, but they are different. They expect some participants to interpret – that limits how much they can take part. You can't assume that people using BSL (British Sign Language) and Sign Supported English are the same and that at a pinch one will do for the other. The first course for interpreters is just starting. We only know of two black signers.'

There is growing awareness among local authorities serving multi-racial communities of the need to provide competent, trained interpreters to meet statutory obligations and provide an effective and equitable service to people with limited English. The director of a project offering training for ethnic minority interpreters said:

'Workers can get used to getting by without an interpreter, people deluding themselves they're doing OK. It's easy in a relationship like social services where you have a lot of power, to think everything is OK. You feel you're getting through, the client is sitting there nodding. You don't see them except in that situation, maybe talking in English to a limited degree. People are reluctant to communicate in such situations, frightened, uncertain, feelings of prejudice, language difficulties. So the worker may see very little. Unless they have the opportunity to see a client speaking in their own language or with an interpreter, quite often they don't get to know what they are missing. We've developed a code of practice for interpreters which the local authority has accepted. For instance, if the client is in conflict with the department, they are told they are free to obtain an independent interpreter.

The need for full-time interpreters can be linked to racist recruitment policies, so it's got to be looked at in terms of long-term recruitment planning. Here there's a positive action plan in the social services department to reach 30 per cent Asian and Afro-Caribbean staff. Turnover of staff is quite high so you can make the change. We're setting up a trainee scheme to enable members of ethnic minorities to become social workers. In times of short resources, agencies are reluctant to advertise themselves for fear of being deluged, but this of course works against groups who under-use them. It certainly calls for targeted information. The better a service is, the more people are likely to get to know about it on the grapevine, which is probably more effective anyway.'

Good translation is important and may be expensive. It brings with it complex decisions. For example:

'Do you have a leaflet translated as it is? This runs the risk that the people reading it may not fully understand it. It won't necessarily mean anything to them as their culture is different. It might even offend them. Instead it might be translated in culturally familiar terms, explaining why such a service has come about and is necessary in this country and explaining why projects and management structures work as they do in Britain. It needs thought and training.'

Four elements of equal opportunities policy have been identified in social services. They relate to both service delivery and employment:

● **equal access** – efforts are made to bring down barriers and open up communication
● **equal shares** – a quantitative measure: the proportion of people using services reflects their particular needs and characteristics and the proportion employed in them reflects their skills and numbers
● **equal treatment** – a qualitative measure: service users and workers are treated appropriately and are not disadvantaged or discriminated against because of their membership of a minority group

● **equal outcomes** – the goal of longer term policy and practice change. (Connelly, 1985)

How, for example, do you ensure access to services for refugees? As the housing and refugees officer of one local authority said:

> **'It appoints someone like me and it makes a commitment to doing something. This authority has instructed its housing officers not to ask people any questions on their refugee status or ask for papers but to take their word. It has to be prepared to listen to refugees. The political will has to be there.'**

Components of equal opportunities programmes include training, support, consultation, funding for independent initiatives, monitoring, reviews, equal opportunities units and forums. Progress is reflected in the wide range of guide-lines now available, to ensure disabled people access to buildings, meetings and conferences, for ethnic record keep-ing and monitoring and for the recruitment and selection of staff. Policies for access and equal opportunities blur into citizen involvement. All the elements of involvement we have identified – information, training, language, forums, struc-tures and so on – should also be checked to ensure equal access and opportunities. Otherwise they will merely reflect the wider oppressions people face because of their age, race, sex, class, disability or sexual orientation. There is no excuse for excluding anyone.

A worker with a project offering intensive support to people with learning difficulties with an additional physical or sensory disability and behaviour identified as difficult, said:

> **'We spend a long time getting to know someone and trying out various things with them. The idea is that the person is able, perhaps for the first time, to choose what they would like to do and to be given information about what kind of choices are available. We are producing an activities folder which will consist of photographs of various activities to give**

**people an idea of what they'd like and to help people who
have no verbal communication to select things they'd like to
try.'**

The involvement of children

The idea of involving children raises very strong feelings, both
for and against. This is particularly true in the context of
social services and child protection. In Britain the 1989
Children Act gives a new prominence to children's own
wishes and feelings in decision-making that affects them. It
places a duty upon social services to consult with them. Ideas
about the involvement of children have been influenced by
thinking about child development as well as legal frameworks.
Chronological age is notoriously unreliable as an indicator of
children's ability to participate. Research into children's
intellectual, social and emotional development increasingly
suggests that they can make a contribution about how they
are treated and what they want from a very early age.
However this does not always sit comfortably with prevailing
values about childhood and children's rights.

Different children and children of different ages may be
able to participate in different ways and to different degrees,
but then the same is true for adults. There is strong evidence
to support greater involvement by children and young people
in decision-making. What it requires is particular sensitivity to
how children are involved and what support they are offered.
The rights of children are especially vulnerable. This is an
added reason to involve them, not to exclude them (Hodgson,
1992).

Forums and structures for involvement

Participatory structures and forums aren't the only expression
of citizen involvement. It may be reflected in an agency's
overall culture and our day-to-day dealings with it. But the
part they play is central. They are the setting for most
attempts to gain more say in services and neighbourhoods.

Their dynamics have a major bearing on the nature of that participation. This is where individuals, organisations and the idea of involvement ultimately meet. One reluctant participant told us:

'If I am ill, I want to be properly treated, but I don't necessarily want to join the Community Health Council.'

True, but one day he might decide he needs to, to get the treatment he prefers. If we want a say, even if we just want decent services, we may not be able to avoid these institutions. That's why it's important to understand them. They include all sorts of structures, from local authority consultative committees, to international pressure groups. It's helpful to draw some distinctions.

They may be located within or outside agencies, be independent or part of them, like the tenants' panel set up by the housing department and the tenants association trying to exert pressure on it. Sometimes the line is blurred because agencies fund or initiate external arrangements. User groups are increasingly being set up in this way. The focus may be a single department or extend across agencies. Consultative arrangements for joint care planning for community care bring together health and social services, statutory and voluntary organisations.

Forums may be for one group, for example, a patients' council or carers' consultation, or mixed, like the governing body of a school which includes politicians, professionals and parent governors. Mixed groups raise important issues for participants who may feel outnumbered and overwhelmed. Participatory groups and structures may be open, like the organisation of people with mental distress which has many 'allies' – professionals who share its philosophy – among its members, or separatist, like the local disability forum which disabled people decided should be closed to able-bodied participants and observers.

Different structures have been developed for different settings. In social services, for instance, residents' committees have been established in old people's homes and student councils in adult training centres for people with learning difficulties. One department set up a group to explore policy and practice issues for people with AIDS, chaired by the deputy director and including social workers, home helps and members of self-help groups.

Participatory arrangements in local government are based both on their administrative and political systems. Departments set up planning groups and advisory committees. People may be co-opted to council committees, either as individuals or representatives of organisations. Some councils have set up disability, women and ethnic minority subcommittees, which include co-opted representatives.

The structures used by statutory and non-statutory organisations may be different. In statutory agencies, they are ultimately tied to the democratic process. Voluntary organisations are often run by management committees. Inviting users of services to join these has increasingly been seen as a way of achieving user-involvement. A project we visited which aims to raise the voice of older women, was run as a collective by its members and two paid workers.

Structures may be organised according to use of a particular agency or service, or around a particular group or issue, like the local authority participation steering group for people with learning difficulties, which one of us was involved in setting up.

There are many different ways of achieving the same end. For instance, one decentralised council has a variety of consultative arrangements linked to its new neighbourhood committees. In one there is a neighbourhood forum elected by proportional representation. Another has two consultative subcommittees, whose co-opted members include representatives from trade unions and tenants associations. In a third each tenants' and residents' association has a representative on the advisory committee.

All participatory structures and forums have their pros and cons. However, they seem to have two things in common.

● they place a premium on group work skills; and
● they are formal structures, with their own culture, rules and ways of working, even if they try and operate informally.

Both of these characteristics have far-reaching implications for people's participation. Forums may be complex and highly structured. For instance we visited a borough forum for older people which aims to be 'a parliament for pensioners'. It meets every two months and is open to all local old people. When we went, two hundred people, including some who were very old, were feeding back their comments on proposed cuts in social services. The forum has a management committee, elected at its annual general meeting, which meets monthly. This has reserved places for women and members of minority ethnic communities, two co-opted councillor members and three from voluntary organisations. The forum's part-time worker is accountable to it and funded by the local authority – one of the agencies it aims to influence. Five officers elected by the management committee make up the officers committee. They meet monthly a week before the management committee to prepare its business.

The council has set up a pensioners' subcommittee of the social services committee which meets quarterly and includes the five officers of the forum as co-opted members. The forum is also affiliated to a metropolitan 'forum for the elderly', 'a non-party political campaigning organisation'. Two of its officers are on the executive committee, which consists of 25 elected representatives as well as non-voting co-opted members.

We can get some idea of what participatory structures actually feel like from snapshots of people's own experience. This young woman was co-opted to a council childcare review subcommittee as representative of an organisation for young people leaving care.

> **'I go to meetings to get what I want. I don't have the time to go to these meetings and just sit there with nothing specific. I go knowing what I want because councillors go knowing what *they* want. I'm afraid you have to play the game or else you're out of it. When I go down to the town hall I'm something of a novelty. When they want to hear what I say, they hear. When they don't, they don't. One of the other**

co-opted members is also a black woman and she's a support to me. I go because I want to learn. No I can't really say I enjoy it. I feel it's one of these things I've got to go through. It's where the power is. Since I've been on it, I've helped make a lot of changes, like getting a girl in bad conditions in a secure unit out, getting her to come to the committee and presenting her own report. Things written about her presented her as a real monster. What would make it better is getting listened to all the time, not just when they feel like it.'

Members of an umbrella organisation of disabled people talked about their local authority disability subcommittee.

'The regular meetings we have with social services, for instance, are helpful. The subcommittee is useless. Most of the disabled people who sit on it are connected with us in one way or another. It's often a repeat for us of other meetings. It slows things down if decisions are sent to it. If they aren't making decisions elsewhere, then maybe we'll think we'd better send it off to disability. We thought it would be a good idea as it's directly under policy and resources [committee]. Then disability wouldn't just be seen as a matter of social services. It doesn't have any money of its own. There's no strong commitment and it's not well attended by councillors. The chair is a dragon and some officers have built a strong defence against her. What's difficult is for disabled people themselves to challenge that.'

'It's very inhibiting The first six meetings the only people who spoke were two other councillors diametrically opposed to the chair and it was a slanging match. Disabled people felt intimidated and didn't know the procedure. You're supposed to say who you are but people don't. The whole tenor of it was patronising. It was some time before we felt we should be involved in it. We have access to the agenda. We can put our items on it. As an organisation we prefer not to take things to the committee as it slows them down.'

Language

Language raises many issues for involvement. Central is its relation with power. Language is not neutral. Feminists have argued that it's man-made and a field of conflict. People with physical disabilities show how it is used to handicap and oppress them. Labels like 'the old', 'the unemployed', 'the mentally ill' are imposed upon people. When people want to be treated on their own terms, for example, as having learning difficulties rather than being 'mentally handicapped', they can expect strong resistance. Language is inseparable from power. It reflects inequalities and must change if they are to be challenged. One American music star tells how during his life he has been described as the first negro, coloured and now black country and western singer! What is valued one day may be devalued the next. So long as identities are devalued, the terms attached to them will constantly be changing. So long as people identify themselves or are identified as a group, we should use the labels *they* prefer. There isn't always agreement. This demands even more sensitivity, not less. The only course consistent with empowerment is for people to define their own terms.

A professional writing the report of a search conference commented:

> **'It is important to say that language was a particular problem . . . Some professionals can only talk in mystifying jargon or in language which many service users find offensive. One of the terms, for example, which some service users objected to during the Conference was "mental health" which they feel to be meaningless. We have, however, chosen to use it in this Report because we want people who use such terms to read it and perhaps reflect more deeply on the issue of language.'**

But isn't this the kind of argument that's been used to justify the continued use of racist and sexist language?

We may be betrayed by the language we're used to. Service providers have traditionally controlled the language of welfare. Take the term 'client' in social work. It's not only contentious because of the inequality it implies. It also helps keep people at arm's length as a separate group. Practitioners talk about 'my clients', implying an ownership they should not have.

If it's jargon, discriminatory or unfamiliar, language can exclude as well as demean. At an international tribunal for poor women in which one of us took part, one British woman said that she didn't know what the word 'plenary' meant in the programme. She had asked some friends who didn't know either. Thus one group is overpowered by the language of another.

Involvement raises language issues of its own. In social services, for instance, the talk is now of customers and consumers as well as clients. People should be cautious about adopting such consumerist terms unless they accept the ideological baggage that goes with them. We have also been told that families using a local family centre did not like the term 'user' because of its drug associations. It has been tarnished in the same way in the USA. Some disabled people and recipients of mental health services also reject the term 'user' because they do not wish to be defined in terms of services which they find oppressive. This again makes the case for leaving the last word on language to the people involved themselves. Our preference, as we said earlier, is for an emphasis on people as *citizens,* not users or consumers; on service use not as a status but as an activity carrying with it civil rights and responsibilities.

Changing language is unlikely to solve anything on its own. It must be seen as part of a parcel of change. We can expect many organisations to learn a new rhetoric for involvement as they have for race and gender, while their policy and practice remain essentially the same. We should beware of 'talking a good service' but doing little else.

Advocacy

Advocacy is central to any discussion of involvement and empowerment. It can give people a say they have previously been denied and turn paper entitlements into real rights. Five kinds of advocacy are identified. Four of these are concerned with speaking on *someone else's* behalf. The other, self-advocacy is concerned with speaking for *yourself*. We introduced the idea in the last chapter.

Self-advocacy is one of the themes of this book. It means people speaking *for themselves* and asserting their own rights, both as individuals and in groups with shared experiences or beliefs. The term came into use during the 1980s. Self-advocacy has been an important and influential idea. It has played a central part in developments and discussions about user-involvement. Four different kinds of self-advocacy groups have been identified, from autonomous groups independent of professional services or parent bodies, like People First, to those which are part of the service system, for example, adult training centre committees and residents' groups in hospitals and residential provision. Self-advocacy is concerned both with people's personal and political needs, offering warmth, friendship and support as well as teaching social skills and representing people's interests in local and national affairs.

The idea of self-advocacy, however, does raise a number of problems. It's worth looking at these in more detail because they highlight some of the difficulties which face people who try to gain more say and control in their lives and over the services they use. Growing concerns have been expressed that self-advocacy has been trivialised and neutralised by services. Steve Dowson highlighted some of the problems in a report called 'Keeping It Safe' (Dowson, 1990):

● The idea of self-advocacy started with professionals   and service providers and ownership of it remains with them. Many self-advocacy groups are run by service providers.
● The term 'self-advocacy' is itself part of the professional jargon which people involved in user groups are trying to challenge.
● Attaching such a special label to people's efforts to gain more control over their lives has resulted in it being treated as something which only happens at special times and in special places, instead of being part of their ordinary lives. Self-advocacy becomes just another activity people have to do at the social education centre,

instead of them being able to say what they want and this being taken seriously all the time.

● Self-advocacy becomes a talking shop. It is restricted to mean people speaking for themselves instead of them also having the chance to take action to fight for their rights.

● Self-advocacy becomes a delaying tactic. Essential changes are made to wait on the development of a self-advocacy group.

The idea of self-advocacy has brought about some valuable gains in citizen involvement and many professionals have tried to support it in a positive way. But it does seem to have some particular shortcomings of its own as well as reflecting a more general problem – that service systems tend to try and keep control and undermine the efforts of service users to gain a greater voice. What it does do is emphasise the importance of each of us being able to speak for ourselves and say what we want, instead of someone else doing this for us. It also offers an important reminder that this must be coupled with action, if people are to achieve self-determination. Many organisations of disabled people talk about *self-organisation* rather than self-advocacy.

Now let's turn to the four forms of advocacy concerned with speaking on *someone else's* behalf. These are:

Legal advocacy – lawyers and others with legal training assist people to exercise or defend their rights, for example, through a local law centre or representation project in a psychiatric hospital.

Professional advocacy – professionals with welfare rights and other skills offer people support and advice to deal with services like income maintenance, housing and social services. Two associated developments in social services are *service brokerage* and *case* or *care management*. With service brokerage, the broker acts as an agent, offering information and advice and negotiating on behalf of a disabled person for the purchase of service through individually allocated funding. This is done with the support of the individual's family and friends. If there isn't a support network, one may be set up which includes a citizen advocate. Case or care management is also concerned with designing 'care packages'. In one model that has been developed in Britain, the case manager is independent of service providers and accountable to the service user, offering independent advocacy and coordinating individually tailored packages of care.

Lay or citizen advocacy – the idea of lay advocates is long established. More recently citizen advocacy has emerged from the United States where it was first used with people with learning difficulties. It rests on a set of clear principles:

> **'A valued citizen who is unpaid and independent of human services creates a relationship with a person who is at risk of social exclusion and chooses one or several of many ways to understand, respond to and represent that person's interests as if they were the advocate's own thus bringing their partner's gifts and concerns into the circles of ordinary community life.'** (O'Brien, 1987)

Advocates are selected and trained to work on a one-to-one basis, in long term relationships, with chosen partners. Their primary loyalty must be to their partners and they are backed up by coordinating staff. The advocacy office should be independent from service providers in administration, location and funding.

Peer advocacy – where people advocate for others with similar experience.

One survey suggests three levels of advocacy (Good Practices in Mental Health, 1986):

● **informal advocacy**, setting out the options for individuals and negotiating on their behalf;
● **formal advocacy**, taking up issues for individuals and pursuing them through administrative complaints procedures, tribunals and the courts
● **public or collective advocacy**, taking up issues which affect more than one individual, at local and national level, lobbying and negotiating with agencies and government for changed practice, policy and legislation.

Three shared characteristics have been identified in effective advocacy projects:

● **independence** of service providers
● **accessibility**, with convenient opening hours, accessible location and a pro-active approach
● **competence**, through proper training and support for staff.

We take for granted people's right to be legally represented. But the right to advocacy still does not exist in many other situations where it is no less important. For example, in Britain, one of the as yet unrealised objectives of the 1986 Disabled Person's Act was to give people a right for the first time to be represented in their dealings with government agencies.

It is also important that other forms of advocacy are complementary to self-advocacy, rather than an alternative to it. There is an emphasis, for example, on citizen advocacy being linked with self-advocacy.

However, there may be conflicts here. At their heart, the new movements for citizen involvement represent a move away from professional to self-advocacy; from speaking on people's behalf to making it possible for them to speak for themselves. It's a larger step than is sometimes realised. Some of the best and most valued work of both statutory and voluntary welfare organisations has been in the field of professional advocacy. Enabling people to speak and act for themselves demands a very different approach and new skills for human service agencies. Making the change, as some are now trying to do, can be an uncomfortable and bruising experience. The culture of professional advocacy is a difficult one to shake off and individuals and agencies may not always be aware when they have not fully succeeded. Much can be gained from speaking on other people's behalf: skills, status, recognition and good feelings. It may be difficult to give these up.

We'd like to highlight three other issues advocacy raises:

● Beware the argument that 'there will always be some people' who can't speak for themselves. Perhaps, but we have yet to meet them! Other people's experience bears this out. For example:

'The person who assertively expresses a concern to a staff person, even non-verbally, may be practising as significant an act of self-advocacy as another who speaks knowledgeably to a legislator.' (Shearer, 1986, p. 180)

'The most profoundly handicapped people, may with help as required, attend meetings and lend support by their presence.' (Williams and Shoultz, 1982)

Ways have been found to help people participate who have limited movement, speech, communication or intellectual abilities. Modern electronic aids, visual games and other techniques have been used. Instead of just assuming that people can't speak for themselves, the onus should be on proving that expert skills and support are as yet insufficient to enable them to.

● A clear distinction should be drawn between advocacy and service provision. This is increasingly an issue for voluntary agencies which have traditionally served an advocacy role, but have now also become large scale service providers.
● It's crucial that having an advocate doesn't become just another legitimating hoop people must go through. This merely disadvantages those who aren't represented, confirming people's powerlessness and the low value placed on them. Studies showed that regardless of their case, people were more likely to win supplementary benefit appeal tribunals if they were represented. More recently research has highlighted the importance of representation at *all* kinds of tribunals (Genn and Genn, 1989).

This emphasises the dilemma for practitioners trying to act as advocates. Social workers, for example, were advised to act as 'determined advocates' for clients seeking a grant or loan from the Social Fund. But how would they avoid being sucked into the Social Fund system themselves? This is a long-standing quandary for social workers; often having to present their clients in dependent and negative terms in order to get something for them. The director of a campaigning organisation working with people with learning difficulties raised another equally important point:

> 'One of the unfortunate effects I've noticed of citizen advocacy is that it can be taken by professionals as allocating all concern for the user's rights to one individual – and so letting everybody else off the hook. Thus I've noticed in the course of acting as an advocate at case conferences some usually enlightened professionals have left me to do all the work of arguing for the person. The ability of service workers to know and protect the user's interests may be imperfect, but they have a duty to try.'

These issues highlight the importance of a two pronged approach: challenging arrangements which devalue what people themselves have to say, as well as supporting them to speak for themselves.

5

Guidelines for Involvement: The Agency Perspective

'When children are assessed for mobility, they try to do all they can, when what they should be showing is how *little* they can do, like in a court for damages. You have to go and get nappies for your adolescent child. There's nowhere to park. You have to sign the form each time. A new assessment is made every time you need a new size. Our children are never the problem. It's the *services*. Whatever you need, however small, you know you've got a battle on.'

'My services have never been altered by any of the suggestions that have been made. We're on the steering group. We're supposed to be involved in staff selection. But it doesn't seem to mean much. The manager has decided that the respite care centre should be closed. Instead the children go on outings. It's just one thing they've decided, replacing another. We get outvoted at staff selection. He just employs clones of himself and now after running it down, he's off to another job.'

How can people's involvement be effective and not just reinforce their sense of powerlessness, as with these parents of disabled children and children with learning difficulties? In this chapter we want to outline a set of guidelines which will help make this possible. They provide an agenda both for people trying to gain a greater say and for agencies and organisations which want to offer it. These are the criteria that go through *our* minds before we accept any invitations to get involved. Again it is not a definitive list, but it provides an initial inventory for action. It can't guarantee people's participation, but we have seen few successful initiatives where these principles have not been present.

Citizen involvement is not an exact science. There is still much to learn. But a lot of experience has been gained. There's no excuse for ignoring this and doing it badly. It's not enough for agencies to have their hearts in the right place. They must couple this with an understanding of the issues and principles involved.

Before we discuss these guidelines in more detail, let's look at a list of them. They are in no particular order. None has any special priority. Each has its own importance.

> Clarify what kind of involvement is on offer
> ● Involve people from the start
> Make clear the limits of involvement
> Provide safeguards for people's involvement
> Set small but attainable goals for change
> Build in involvement as part of the agency structure and process
> ● Establish a continuing process of involvement
> Make specific provision for the involvement of minority ethnic communities
> Develop appropriate forms and forums
> Allow people's involvement to be flexible and open-ended
> Ensure involvement is by choice, not compulsion
> Involve all the key participants concerned
> Give priority to people's own accounts of their wants and needs.

Clarify what kind of involvement is on offer

Earlier we argued that agencies should be clear whether they really want people's involvement and why they want it. They must also decide what *kind* of involvement they want: information-gathering, consultation or a direct say in decision-making. So, for example, as one local authority wrote to us:

> '**A joint activist and departmental group produced a report on participation way back which got shelved . . . It has surfaced again in a report written by an outside consultant . . . The report makes clear the Department has not thought through the issues in any real depth – particularly the distinction between participation, information-giving, consultation and control.**'

Any confusion here is likely to be as damaging as a lack of commitment. Each of these approaches is valid. Each can offer benefits to both citizens and agencies. But they are very different. Their implications for agencies are also very different. Once people have a direct say, the initiative passes from the agency. This can lead to profound change in both its nature and purpose.

So far in discussions about 'giving a voice to the consumer', we have heard most rhetoric about democratising services. Most interest seems to have been expressed in consultation and generally we have not got much beyond information-gathering. Information-gathering often masquerades as consultation, and consultation as a direct say. Whichever they opt for, agencies should let people know. If they are not yet sure, they should say so. So long as people labour under misapprehensions and assume that any call for their views automatically means they will be acted upon, then the outcome is likely to be more disappointment and distrust.

Involve people from the start

Agencies should start as they mean to go on. If they want to involve people then they should try to do so at the earliest possible opportunity. It's essential if there's to be any chance of an equal and effective dialogue. Then people can gain a sense of ownership in developments and not feel they are being offered something where the choices have been made, options closed and the crucial decisions already reached. Why should they get involved in other people's plans? The reality is that most won't want to. Take this development officer.

'My brief is to find premises and finance for a mental health centre and to approach potential users to find out what kind of a service they would like. There's a commitment on the part of the steering group to user involvement . . . There used to be a couple of users involved on it, but they fell away. They were probably a bit overwhelmed by how much there was to do and the lack of provision and help for them. I'm hoping to set up a pilot project next year, hiring a room to run a drop in/advice centre twice a week . . . I like the day centres I've seen that have an "informal" model with some structured activities. People can go to the centre, have a snack, a cup of tea, a chat, whatever they want and join in other activities, for example, a woman's group.'

But say people don't want to go to a segregated centre? What chance will they have to develop other ideas and put them on the agenda? There's a clear contradiction here between asking people what service they want and deciding beforehand on a day centre.

Once the process has begun, it becomes increasingly difficult either to stop or change it. It develops its own momentum, dynamics and direction. The balance of power, interests and subgroups will all be significantly shaped by its initial design. The greater the delay before people are drawn in, the more likely it is that the agendas of those initiating the exercise will predominate. Broad-based involvement is more difficult to engender the longer it is left.

There are many tensions and ambiguities. Is it right to involve people before we even know if the resources are there to go ahead? Is it fair to involve them from the beginning when the whole process could take years? But aren't they the best judges of this? Asking them and putting them properly in the picture will at least give people the chance to decide for themselves. It may also suggest a strategy for dealing with some of these difficulties. Take the dilemma described by a member of staff of a new under-fives centre.

'Once the staff knew where the nursery was going to be, they leafleted the immediate local area. We knew that we couldn't leaflet the whole estate as it would be unfair. We knew we could only have 15 children and to leaflet the whole area would raise unfair expectations. At an initial meeting we involved some local parents in working out what the catchment area of the nursery would be exactly. Some people who live just out of the catchment area are very resentful when they find that out and are told they cannot have a place.'

Wouldn't it have made more sense to involve everyone from the start? It might have been painful for both parents and staff. But it could also have been constructive. In the event, excluding people from discussion about the catchment area perpetuated rather than resolved the problem.

Practical and personal arguments can always be offered for delaying people's involvement. But before acting on them, agencies and practitioners should ask themselves two questions.

● Are we sure we aren't patronising people?
● What might this say about our own reluctance to relinquish control?

Make clear the limits of involvement

There will always be limits to involvement. What is important is to make these clear. Inviting parents to case conferences does not mean they have a vote in deciding whether their child has been abused, but it does give them a chance to put their case and see what's happening. There are areas and issues where an agency or public service cannot and perhaps for legal reasons is not allowed to hand over powers. There are also values which may not be negotiable. For example, proposals which discriminate against women, members of minority ethnic communities or elderly people will not be accepted.

Agencies and workers must make clear what is and is not negotiable. Then people can decide whether they want to go ahead on these terms or perhaps contest them. Organisations should explain which decisions are within their power, which people have a say in and what resources are available. They should never assume other people know something just because they themselves do. Community workers set up a tenants' group in our flats to get the repairs done. When council notices were served, the landlord sold out. Now the whole process had to start again. 'Oh, that's a regular tactic they use', the community worker explained. One of our neighbours said:

> **'I just wish I'd never got involved in all this. If they'd have told us what it would be like at the time, I'd have kept out of it. All I wanted was my home to be nice. They got the builders in. All the plaster's chipped off my walls for damp proofing and the skirting boards are off and they've just taken the men off the job. What am I supposed to do with a small baby, and rats getting in? I was better off before.'**

The fullest possible information should be provided in accessible forms. Agencies may not have all the data they need. Circumstances change. If so, let people know. If this doesn't happen, participants are left in a quandary: reluctant to jettison the work they have already done, but unwilling to throw good money after bad. Agencies should communicate their aims, constraints and timescales openly and honestly from the very beginning so that people can know as soon as possible what they are letting themselves in for and what they might want to challenge. This is the only way any of us can make a rational decision about getting involved.

Provide safeguards for people's involvement

> **'They ask your opinion and then they go and do what they were going to in the first place.'**

If agencies want people's involvement they must offer commitments and safeguards. Why should people get involved if all that's on offer is a vague undertaking to 'hear their views'?

We know this is one of the reasons why involvement tends to be limited and biased.

Some social services departments have introduced 'users' charters'. These give people a right to be consulted, but no guarantee that they will be listened to. Young people in care have a statutory right to be consulted, but most seem to feel it gives them little say.

In some settings such rights are well-established. Local people on the management committees of community associations decide what activities to offer and whom to employ. Some neighbourhood forums have control over small budgets. Self-run services, like this local authority-funded day service for psychiatric service users have built-in safeguards for people's involvement.

> **'Here you're in charge . . . If it's a committee meeting, staff can come in by invitation. They can't be on the committee. The executive committee and Monday meetings are the way for members of the group to have a say . . . We've got a constitution.'**

We haven't encountered many examples of information-gathering or consultation where such undertakings are made. But there are some helpful models. For instance, participatory research:

> **'Instead of disappearing with their data, the researcher says "we'll come back to you with the report. You can change it. You've got control over the process." It's agreed.'**

This is how workers producing a health pack for groups of older people and people working with them sought to safeguard their involvement.

> **'We had an advisory group with members of local pensioners' groups on it. We took it to lots of groups. We tried it out with them and made changes. It took a year or so. There was a lot of to-ing and fro-ing. It worked very well. Loads of pensioners' groups turned up when we launched it. They felt involved and very positive about it.**

We're going back now with questionnaires to find out if people have used it, what bits they used, how they found it, what changes they'd recommend. We want to set up an editorial group including them. We've got funding for group meetings, to meet with people who've commented on it, if they've got time, to advise us.'

Sometimes people can secure commitments instead of being offered them, like this local association of disabled people.

'We do a lot of work on access. We go through all the planning applications. We write to developers, meet with borough and private developers, go to site meetings. We can point to buildings all over the borough that have substantially changed because of this. They're coming to us now. It's the result mainly of lobbying the planning committee. We've worked up quite an effective lobby with committee members . . . We have officers who know that if they go to the planning committee without our support, they'll be thrown out. Members will give them a rough time because we'll give *them* a rough time. Private developers contact us because they know the council wants it.'

But when involvement is invited, commitments should not be seen as something to be given or extracted *after* the process has begun. They should be there from the start. Even when they have been made, there may be a struggle to ensure they are honoured. Without them, people who remain involved can expect a long-drawn-out struggle with ever-diminishing returns. Why should an agency be reluctant to reassure them with firm commitments if it is genuinely prepared to listen to what they say? By making commitments it can begin to develop credibility, establish a track record and build trust. Of course agencies can rarely do what everybody wants. But they can make their criteria clear. For example:

● Has a decision already been made?
● Who is going to hear what people have to say?
● What status will they give it?

What other information and opinions will they consider alongside it?
How will this process be monitored?
How will it be explained to people?

There's also a set of issues for potential participants to consider:

What commitments have been made?
What rights does this involvement offer us?
Can we realise those rights?
What have we been able to achieve from being involved?

Set small but attainable goals for change

This is a plea for small beginnings. It's important to set modest but attainable goals. Involving people is likely to take longer and demand more skills and resources than we expect. We are bound to make mistakes. But starting small means we can build on existing relationships, groups and affiliations. It doesn't railroad people into the relentless timetables of large project planning. Small-scale projects are much more likely to match people's initial expectations and abilities and provide a base from which to develop. Large-scale initiatives fly in the face of the massive political and economic constraints that govern our lives and institutions. Starting small gives us a chance to develop our capacity to challenge such obstacles. People can keep pace and stay in control with a series of small steps. Large leaps are excluding and alienating. It is easy to build on small successes, difficult to overcome large failures.

> 'The council put forward a community space initiative. Two officers came to the tenants' association meeting and asked for people's ideas. The three of us suggested a playspace. Eventually they offered the site at a peppercorn rent and gave us £300 and two hundredweight bags of grass seed – which the pigeons ate! Then we got a grant. If we'd been realistic about what we'd been doing we'd never have done it! We thought it was a matter of throwing grass seed down. We didn't know

how to dig up the fence posts left from the prefabs. We didn't know how to stop people dumping. We had meetings about everything.'

All the pressures seem to be for more ambitious and prestigious projects. Modest proposals may be more effective, but they are less likely to bring status to agencies and authorities. Managers and politicians want quick results. Experiments are expected to be showpieces, instead of being able to admit their difficulties and failures. Workers in the middle can quickly become jaundiced and disillusioned. Potential participants stay on the sidelines.

We need to redefine what's big and what's small. Some goals may seem humble, like giving people control over a small sum of money or the design of one small service. But they can represent a major achievement by:

● overcoming people's suspicion
● changing their expectations of being ignored
● demonstrating that citizen involvement is a practical policy
● showing people that they can do it.

Initiatives that gain confidence and trust have a significance far beyond their size.

'Social workers had gone to people on the estate before and talked about what they wanted. Nothing had ever come of it. This time, they told us they wanted a holiday scheme and it was set up through the community association. It was great. But it was much more than that. For the first time something had happened. It made a real change in how they saw us. It changed the relationship between local people and social services.'

Build in involvement as part of the agency structure and process

Citizen involvement is not something that can just be tagged on to the existing structure of agencies. This is true, whatever kind of involvement is on offer, if there is a genuine commitment to listen to what people say. It demands a different way of working, not an addition to existing procedures. It's the inability or unwillingness of agencies to accept this that undermines many attempts to involve people. Administrative exercises in participation that aren't connected with the political process quickly founder. People's involvement can't be sought in isolation. It must be integrated with existing structures and arrangements. It must be related to trade union agreements, professional practices, manifesto commitments and council standing orders.

Take this youth centre. First let's listen to a member of its running committee.

> **'The staff keep very much in the background. It's us who make all the overall decisions. The staff really are here to oversee things, to give advice if needed, to help the running committee or members if they need it. The running committee also help appoint staff. The vacancies are advertised. The candidates meet the youth leader and are on trial for a month and are then interviewed by three members of the running committee.'**

This is what the youth leader said:

> **'All part-time youth workers employed in the borough are interviewed and accepted or rejected centrally and then deployed round the borough, so some would come to this youth club that way. I have had it agreed that they can be interviewed by members of the running committee. But the Council don't really accept the authority of the young people in the club. I think the structure giving young people a say here is fairly safe at the moment, but over a long period of time with a youth worker who was not committed to the ideas of empowerment and enabling, then it could be undermined. I'm hoping to set up a management committee for the club which would have 51 per cent of young people so they would have the overall say. I want to get it formally agreed by the Council so that young people's say in the running of the club is secure and guaranteed for the future.'**

Establish a continuing process of involvement

Citizen involvement is likely to be most effective if it is a continuing process. Often it's limited to one-off or sporadic events like open days, workshops, public meetings and sample surveys. These may offer brief flashes of illumination, but they can also echo our experience of party politics – visible at election time and then quickly disappearing. Continuing processes and structures, such as neighbourhood committees and regular consultation exercises, make it possible for people's familiarity, confidence and trust to grow. For example, a consumers group of people aged sixty and over, 'the thousand elders', was set up to test products, participate in experiments and answer questionnaires. Community architects on a council estate opened an office on site and held weekly meetings with tenants' representatives and housing officers to work out what improvements to make. They concluded:

> 'To be successful, participation must be an on-going dialogue, extending over a considerable period of time, based on individual commitment and respect between all the interested parties, drawing out the best from each in a constant and ever-questioning search for better ways of doing things.'
> (Thompson, 1985)

This is especially important given the different ways we use services. That raises two important issues:

- How can people be involved in planning and running services if they only use them briefly or occasionally?
- How do you avoid the involvement of one group or generation of users prescribing the service another receives?

Social services highlight the difficulties. We may live permanently in sheltered accommodation or use a lunch club regularly. Here relationships can develop and opportunities for unforced contact are plentiful. But we may only have a social worker for a short time or be offered respite care infrequently. We may come to social services unexpectedly and at a time of crisis.

First, services must be flexible so they can adapt to individual needs. Second, they should facilitate people's involvement in the ways we discuss in this book, so it can develop over a short time. Finally, there should be open forums with a changing membership as well as regular testing and monitoring so that people's ideas and experience can be incorporated and services constantly modified according to shifting patterns of use, wants and satisfaction. Later we shall be looking at some of the problems of maintaining continuing involvement and how these can be overcome.

Make specific provision for the involvement of minority ethnic communities

Ethnic minority organisations continue to report social and other services which are not reaching or are inappropriate for their communities. For example:

> **'Social service departments have, to date, failed in their statutory duties to help "vulnerable people" in the black communities . . . Consultation with the black communities in the past has been non-existent or cosmetic. If black people are to start having any faith in these consultation processes, the consultation procedures must be on-going and use a variety of approaches. Any consultation process must have built in evaluation and monitoring systems.**
>
> **There are ground rules. Do all users have information, in language they understand, in spoken language, not just on paper, about how they can get services, and advice and explanation of their rights?'** (Dutt, 1990)

A black trainer told us:

> **'If a service is set up for the local community, it's got to be controlled together with that local community, black and white. It's important for services to make sure they are**

representing black interests. The onus is on them to find ways of drawing on those networks, to involve the strengths of the black community. Organisations have got to question how they've been operating and work out ways to include the whole community. It means making links with black communities – links that are positive to both sides, discovering what people want from those services and not assuming that black people want the same as white people.'

Similar issues face both service providers and service user and rights organisations trying to involve black people and members of other minority ethnic communities. It is essential to make *specific provision* to involve members of ethnic minorities. It is not enough to assume that they will get involved in the general run of participatory initiatives. Experience suggests that this does not happen. Three strategies will help to promote anti-racist policy and practice to involve people. It is important:

● To pay particular attention to the needs of minority ethnic groups in making provision for people's involvement
● To provide resources to help user groups and rights organisations to reach out and involve members of minority ethnic communities
● To give specific support for minority ethnic involvement.

Grant-giving organisations should offer guidance to user and rights organisations to meet their equal opportunities policies. Without this, such demands are likely to be tokenistic.

Develop appropriate forms and forums

For most of us, getting involved still means going to formal meetings or being told to write to our MP or local councillor. It's not surprising if volunteers are often hard to come by. Yet the issue of what forms to use to involve people is rarely on the agenda. They tend to be taken for granted. The most radical causes still sometimes rely on the most traditional ways of working. A large gap continues to exist between people's personal experience and conventional political process.

We haven't come across many examples of innovative ways of involving people. Few participatory initiatives have the time or resources to experiment. It's also often difficult for people who are involved to understand how others may experience methods which they are used to.

Developing forms and forums for involvement is not just a matter of establishing institutions or procedures. As we have seen, there's an enormous variety of such structures, from tenants' panels to community health councils. The real question is how to develop methods of participation that unintentionally or otherwise don't exclude or discriminate against people. Biased approaches to involvement are actually likely to make things worse, extending existing inequalities of access. Even such proposals as having reserved places in community forums for women, disabled people and members of minority ethnic groups may not open the door to more than a tiny minority of people concerned.

Every method of involvement has its advantages and disadvantages. Different people have different preferences. The two of us are happier chatting in someone's living room. Others may feel more at home in an office. What we can say is that many people are put off by the emphasis placed on formal verbal and writing skills. Leaden meetings, conducted in 'committeespeak', with much passing of paper, are alienating and excluding. Procedural democracy can actually act against many people's participation.

It's not always obvious which methods work best. For instance, one American study suggested that people felt more comfortable with formal than informal arrangements because they then knew where they were (Mansbridge, 1983). We have seen informality used at a supplementary benefit appeal tribunal to catch claimants off-guard. It's important to experiment. Much more work needs to be done to explore and develop appropriate forms of involvement. It's especially important to involve people themselves in shaping the methods used and in finding out which are most effective. There are some bench marks:

● Build on what is familiar in people's lives. There may be lessons to be learned for involving people in formal collective processes from the ways in which they participate in informal shared activities.

● Aim to meet both personal and political needs. Successful methods take into account people's personal needs as well as participatory goals, like the action group for parents with children in care that provides support and speaks up for them.

● Treat people with the consideration we all have a right to expect. Getting involved can be a strain. We have seen people treated badly. People seeking a say in personal services may be under particular difficulties or pressure. It's important to be sensitive to this.

● Involve people on their own terms. Methods of involvement should be acceptable to participants. Before a survey of disabled people was undertaken, relevant organisations were consulted to ensure it was carried out appropriately.

Allow people's involvement to be flexible and open-ended

Being involved shouldn't have to be a full-time occupation, but frequently it is. It's more often a matter of a few people involved in a lot than vice versa. This reflects the nature and culture of involvement in our society. Often it's all or nothing. One woman said to us:

> 'I went to a meeting. People were friendly. I enjoyed it. But there was always pressure to do more. They wanted me to go to more meetings – three or four in one week. Then they said I should stand for secretary. I made excuses and stopped going.'

Involvement must be made more flexible and less demanding. Then people can more readily make small commitments, perhaps for a short time, without feeling trapped. As people have made clear to us, not everyone wants to be involved all the time. People take an active interest in the school when their children are there. They are concerned about their neighbourhood. But it isn't part of a professional or political career. It isn't their abiding interest. They may have children to look after, relationships they cherish, hobbies to pursue and a social life to lead. The membership secretary of a housing cooperative said:

'One woman's got four children and it's difficult for her to come to meetings. I asked her if she could do something indoors. She said, "Yes I'll be delighted." She has a new baby. People do tend to feel you are part of a co-op by coming to meetings. They don't realise you can do it in other ways – like helping out by addressing envelopes.'

Ensure involvement is by choice not compulsion

In our enthusiasm for involvement we should never put pressure on people to participate. It's likely to have the opposite effect, making it just another burden. In one nursery we visited, parents were supposed to come to at least half the meetings of the management committee or they could lose their child's place.

'We haven't enforced this yet but we're going to. We also need voluntary help with cooking, the crêche for the meetings and fundraising. It's always the same people who do the work.'

The effect is divisive. Resentments grow between those who do and those who don't get involved. Participation becomes the price people must pay for an essential service, discriminating against those who have limited access to alternatives. In this case, it particularly discriminated against women, since the responsibility mainly fell on them, yet there might be many reasons why they were unable or unwilling to take part.

The pressures to participate can be subtle and complex. For example at a 'users' rights day' organised by a social services department, an officer working with people using mental health services said:

'Users of mental illness services are here in great support, but they've exerted their rights and don't want to speak this morning . . . Staff expect clients to join in activities, not necessarily all the time, but to achieve objectives . . . I want to talk about the responsibilities towards other people and themselves that go with rights. All choices have consequences. We shouldn't forget that staff also have a right to express their professional judgement. Some kinds of mental illness lead people to withdraw socially and neglect themselves. A lot of work in programmes is done to combat that. There's a clear expectation that people in hostels involve themselves in activities.'

Participation becomes therapy or training and its opposite becomes pathology. The truly therapeutic benefits of empowerment are lost. If people are to have a real choice in whether they get involved:

● participatory initiatives should be checked for any pressures on people to get involved and these pressures removed
● participation should not be a condition of access to scarce services or resources
● all the necessary supports for involvement should be offered
● involvement should not be conceived in therapeutic terms.

Involve all the key participants concerned

All the four key interests involved should have a say in agencies and services: workers, users, indirect users like carers, and other local people. A narrow concern with 'user' or 'consumer' involvement is likely to be divisive and unhelpful. It ignores the overlaps and mutual interests between the four that can be built upon. It may lead us into the consumerist trap where they are often polarised against each other. As a social services trade union official said to us:

'Residents should be asked "What standards of behaviour do
you expect from the staff?" But I think it's also important not
to allow clients to harass staff. A lot of care staff are black
and many residents in their eighties are racist. There's very
few black elderly people in homes and I think staff get racial
harassment. Racist behaviour should be challenged.'

Conceiving of people as 'users' implies it's their sole and
permanent status. It takes no account of the fact that we may
at the same or different times work in a service or use it, care
for and support someone, or need support ourselves. It can
also lead to people being put on a pedestal as if their
pronouncements had a particular legitimacy. Ultimately this
rebounds against them. People using services aren't the sole
repository of truth. They have a special contribution to make.
They are experts in their own experience, but workers and
carers have insights and expertise too.

There will always be differences and conflicts between the
key constituencies of agencies and services. But if any group is
excluded from involvement, it becomes far more difficult to
work through any difficulties. Communication and understanding are undermined.

This became clear at one community nursery. Staff had
complained about an earlier suggestion that only one of them
at a time should come to management committee meetings.
They felt they should be able to come to all of them. Parents
decided at the meeting that the team leader should come every
time and staff on a rota basis. But this wasn't discussed with
staff, who weren't present. A crèche worker requested help as
there were 14 children to look after during the meeting. One
parent said, 'If they are good crèche workers, they should
manage.'

Give priority to people's own accounts of their wants and needs

People are the best judges of their own wants and needs. Their
definitions, not the interpretations of others, are the crucial
ones. They provide one of the keys to:

● move from provider- to user-led services
● match services to people instead of forcing people to fit into services
● start with human instead of organisational issues.

Here's another hierarchy that has to be turned on its head – the hierarchy of credibility attached to people's views and opinions. Much more priority must be given to the ordinary voices of service users, carers and practitioners. This:

● reflects a valuing of what people have to say
● provides crucial information and experience which they alone have.

People are quite capable of offering their own accounts. We have now accumulated many, for example, a gay man describing life after an ileostomy, a woman reporting her experience of manic depression, a resident's inside view of life in an old people's home, and a woman confronting her own death from cancer. They offer an invaluable basis for understanding people's needs and developing agency policy and practice. What people usually lack are access, opportunities and support to produce them. Staff in a project trying to help meet the needs of unemployed young people living in board and lodgings undertook in-depth interviews with them

> 'in direct response to the request of the young people . . . From the beginning they made us aware that they were very anxious to tell their stories.'

A worker with refugees emphasised the responsibility of service providers to:

> 'facilitate service users to present *their* perspective – especially for those whose first language is not English. It helps bridge the gulf between equal access and equal outcomes.'

Developing people's own accounts can take us a long way from traditional information-gathering. They may take many forms: poetry, prose, drama and song.

> **'So open your eyes nurses**
> **Open and see,**
> **Not a crabbit old woman**
> **Look closer – see ME.'**

We have watched videos where young people talk about their experience of being black and in care; where we learn what involving service users in running a voluntary mental health organisation means both for them and for workers, and where a group of people with learning difficulties discuss issues relating to their sexuality. Videos like these are now widely used by both agencies and user groups.

Advocates of reminiscence work with older people point to its importance in understanding their needs as individuals, recognising ethnic and cultural differences and in appreciating people generally in a more holistic way. There's a national magazine by and for young people in care. At a one-day workshop linked to this that we went to, young people in care were able to find out more about producing their own local newsletter, getting together in groups to paste-up a cover in the afternoon.

Some people may be able to produce their own accounts unaided. Some may want some help, for example with writing or making a video. Others may feel more comfortable with someone to put it together for them. Whichever it is, what's crucial is that as far as possible, they *all* have final editorial control over them.

6

Getting Involved with Other People: Moving from Individual to Collective Action

The idea of taking collective action may seem strange to many people. Yet it's something they do all the time. They play team games, look after each other's children or go on holiday together. Often though it conjures up a differe..t set of images, of placards, pickets and demonstrations. The nearest we may have come to them is signing a petition. But there's much more to collective action than these stereotypes suggest. It may mean taking a turn on hospital radio or joining the league of friends, running our own housing or getting together in a residents' association. Trying to have more say in our lives can involve both individual and collective action. Each has its advantages and disadvantages. One may affect the other. If we're to make the best use of either, we need to understand them both. Let's begin with individual action, as most people do.

Individual action

In Western society, acting on your own is the starting point for most people's involvement, since their relationships with organisations and institutions are largely individual. They come to them on their own or in their families. This reflects wider social norms and values.

Westerners learn to look for individual solutions to their problems. That's what they're used to and often it works. If a service is unsatisfactory, they complain; if a product doesn't work, they change it; and if they don't like their neighbourhood, they move. People safeguard their welfare by securing their individual rights. It may not cross their mind to do things any differently. They often only turn to collective action after their individual efforts have failed. There can be different combinations, but a common pattern emerges:

● first try on your own (**individual action**)
● then seek support (**advocacy**)
● finally join forces with others (**collective action**).

We can begin to see some of the issues individual action raises from the comments of this citizen-advocacy coordinator.

'Citizen advocacy is about providing people with someone to represent them. It brings about change because individuals ask for it rather than pressure groups doing it from the top. Being a citizen advocate is essentially individual. It has to be for it to be part of a natural relationship. If one person gets a good deal then others say why haven't we got it. The individual voice has great power. If service providers say to me "if we give it to Mrs Smith we'll have to give it to everyone", I ignore that. I say "I am only concerned with the person I represent".'

Individual action has some potential advantages:

● it is primarily concerned with the individual's own needs and interests
● it can be under their direct control
● it can often achieve small changes successfully for them
● they can speak specifically for themselves
● they don't have to forge new links or negotiate with others.

It can also lead to broader change, as the citizen-advocacy coordinator and a self-advocacy adviser explained:

'While citizen-advocacy focuses on the individual, what we do does change the way services work in the long term. It has spin-offs, for example, creating precedents and as well as working with individuals, collating information and feeding it to agencies.

I can think of individual self-advocates who by their own activity have been able to bring about change in their own locality. At a US conference, I came across the example of a person with learning difficulties who got to know a congressman and as a result got changes for disabled people.'

But there may be deficits too. An emphasis on individual action can:

● **undermine equity** – whether people get their rights and say depends on their individual ability to secure them. Usually only a minority ever have advocates
● **individualise issues** – obscuring the common causes of people's problems and depoliticising them
● **be divisive** – whether one person gets something may depend on somebody else not
● **provide a patchy and piecemeal basis** for developing policy and practice.
●

Collective action

Our personal needs can't all be met individually. Not everything can be solved by trying to tackle problems at the individual level. Disabled people want accessible environments as well as their own personal package of services. The overall shortage of child care services in Britain denies women equal employment opportunities. Racism must be tackled at the institutional as well as the personal level. Collective action helps us both to see and to tackle these broader issues.

We have tried to give some flavour of the diversity of collective action, from ordinary everyday activities to more formal interventions in our services and society. It might mean our involvement in user or community groups, single issue pressure groups or campaigns, or organisations of particular groups of people, like members of minority ethnic groups or disabled people. It encompasses a spectrum of approaches which include **mutual aid**, **negotiation**, **lobbying**, **legal** and **direct action**. This may range from having a quiet word with a councillor we know to taking an authority to an international court. We may use one or all of these, independently or as ascending steps to achieve our objectives.

Collective action poses its own problems. Many of these relate to people's perceptions of it. Some of the key concerns emerging from people we have spoken to who *aren't* involved in collective action are that it:

is unfamiliar
requires new skills
is time consuming
will undermine their privacy by bringing their personal troubles into public view
has negative associations.

But it also has important advantages.

people are more powerful together than on their own
it can bring all the benefits that come from working with other people – pooling skills, providing support, reducing stress and isolation
it offers an effective alternative for people with less individual choice, who can't just move or buy something better
it offers an effective way of bringing about wider change.

Reconciling the two

Individual and collective action reflect different, sometimes conflicting philosophies of self reliance and mutual support. We may feel more comfortable with one than the other. But *both* are essential if people are to have an effective say. One's shortcomings are often the other's strengths. They are closely interdependent. We may gain our individual welfare rights collectively. Sometimes collective action can be best served by an individual test case. There may be tensions between individual rights and collective well-being. That's why it's important to consider *both* approaches in concert. Otherwise one may ride roughshod over the other. We need to be better equipped as individuals to deal with services and policies *and* work collectively to change them. The experience of this community worker with housing groups is typical:

'They'll play people off against each other. They use the individual against the group. By doing something for one person you can shut them up. The "trouble maker" gets things done. Only the loudest voice is listened to. You complain on your own, it tends to focus attention on the failings of front line staff and takes the heat off those who may actually bear responsibility.'

Community development

How can we take the step from individual to collective action? While many of us are involved in voluntary action, we are much less likely to take part in other kinds of collective action about our neighbourhoods or needs. Community development has been the main approach used to encourage people to try. Now agencies are seeing it as a key strategy for 'user involvement'. But it highlights some basic problems in involving people, particularly where one group is attempting to involve another. This, of course, is precisely the position of agencies, activists and development workers who want to increase involvement. The difficulties they face aren't often discussed. The first inkling many may have is when they encounter them first-hand. We need to consider these problems more carefully. They are reflected in three uneasy relationships. These are between:

- change and involvement
- the rhetorical and real scale of involvement
- enabling and organising.

Before turning to these, let's take a closer look at community development. Its main tasks are making contact with people and setting up and supporting groups. It has a long history both with disadvantaged groups and in third-world development. Interest in it has grown as new areas have been identified for collective action and agencies have tried to work in more 'community-orientated' ways. *Community* enterprise, *community* architecture and *community* social work are all examples of this. It offers agencies concerned with user-involvement a way of getting people together, setting up user groups and increasing involvement in consultations.

There are different models of community development. They range from encouraging mutual aid to politicisation, from collaboration to confrontation. They have two common objectives: bringing about change, and involving people in the process. This is where the first tension lies. The two are often difficult to reconcile. The time and resources it takes to involve people effectively often sit uncomfortably with pressures to undertake initiatives or mount campaigns. When one has to be sacrificed, it's usually people's participation. In a frank but rare account of the gulf between participatory rhetoric and community work reality, one development worker described for the first time how agency imperatives, bureaucratic timetables, grant-giving arrangements and the community worker's own culture and needs limit people's involvement. For example:

'In terms of funding this meant that although I had learnt the procedures and didn't like them, I didn't make the step of proposing an alternative, more accessible system. Challenging the grant getting system would also mean that you wouldn't get the money so easily, if at all, and this clashed with my wish to see things set up which were needed . . . I regularly felt frustrated with workers whom I regarded as never getting past the initial discussion stage on anything. I felt that the urgent need for these projects overrode what might be gained if all the emphasis was put on getting active community support for the proposal and by getting others involved in the tedious task of getting funding.' (Mantle, 1985)

This is the development worker's dilemma. If s/he involves people, it may limit what can be done, but if s/he doesn't, what will be achieved anyway? Change isn't just an objective. It must be part of the process. *How* you do it, really is what you get.

That brings us to the second strained relationship. While the rhetoric of community development is of large scale involvement – 'tenants on the estate got together' or 'the local community decided' – the reality is more often one of small groups with little claim to be representative. Broad-based involvement may not even be a central issue on community development's agenda. Take the account of this community development manager we spoke to.

> 'The key activists are your key level. We'd say it is not necessarily the job of the community worker to involve more than a small group of people. You're not a magician. For a community worker, involvement may only be one objective. For example, we focused on one large estate. It had a poor history of trying to set things up. Workers picked up the threads. They set up a youth club group, a group who wanted to set up a community centre and improve heating in the flats, and a community festival and community newspaper group. The numbers involved in the groups were small. The community newspaper went to every house. We know it was valued. There was a festival which ran for two or three years attended by thousands. They got their community centre, improved heating, the youth club. Thirty or forty people were involved. Thousands benefited passively.'

But can narrow involvement be squared with community development's philosophy of giving people a say and starting with *their* definitions of issues? Is it just a coincidence that so many deprived areas have wanted the same package of community festivals, newsletters, centres and youth clubs, or could this tell us something else?

Part of the answer may lie in the last of the issues we identified: the tension between support and direction. This is reflected in community development's own vocabulary. The role of social entrepreneur and organiser, sits uneasily with that of enabler and facilitator. Here we have the development worker as fixer and wheeler-dealer: the person who has contacts in the council, knows how it works and can get things done. What then becomes confused is whether the aim is to pass on these skills to a few others to become the new 'community-' and 'user-leaders', or to try and do things differently by enabling people's involvement. The two need different skills and reflect very different philosophies. The role of development worker is itself almost a contradiction in terms: lively, full of ideas, inspiring others – but always taking a back seat.

Guidelines for community development

These issues place a large question mark over community development approaches. How can we ensure they enable people to set their own agendas and develop their own initiatives instead of imposing others on them? There are real difficulties here. If they aren't recognised and resolved, people may end up as little more than a stage army. It often happens. When a development worker mentioned a self-advocacy group's charter of rights, we overheard one member say, 'Well, you worked them out for us.' Organising people is not the same as involving them. It's not a matter of bad faith, just a host of difficulties between the theory and practice of community development. Its advocates have tended to gloss over the problems of enabling broad-based involvement. But opponents of participation have been quick to criticise people who do get involved, either arguing that they are unrepresentative or suggesting that they have been 'put up to it' in some way.

We need clear guidelines to help us negotiate the pitfalls. For example:

● There are inherent tensions in community development between making change and enabling people's involvement. Enabling broad-based involvement is an essential community development task in itself and not something that can be taken for granted in pursuit of other goals.

The personal and political elements of empowerment must both be addressed. It's important to recognise people's fears and uncertainties about collective action and give them support to increase their confidence and skills.

● Be honest with yourself and others about the difficulties you encounter. Don't pretend they aren't happening. They aren't just your problem. If you have to make trade-offs, be clear about it.

● Identify your own values, agendas, interests and goals and those of the people with whom you are working and distinguish between the two.

● Work to change excluding structures and ways of working. Don't just perpetuate them.

● Own your own role and power; recognise the skills and information you have and never assume that others share them.

● Give people the opportunity to work out their own forms and objectives for involvement and be aware of the danger of unintentionally imposing your own.

● Make realistic assessments with people of what is actually achievable in any given situation; what the possible outcomes are and what the costs may be, so that people can make an informed decision about what they want to do.

● Community development is a difficult and stressful activity. People need personal and professional support to do it properly.

Advisers and allies

The **advisers** and **allies** of self-advocacy groups offer helpful examples of ways of supporting and encouraging people's involvement in collective action, which can deal with some of the difficulties we have discussed. The role of adviser has developed among self-advocacy groups of people with learning difficulties, but it has much wider implications. Guidelines for advisers are already emerging. Independence is clearly important. So is not taking over. This is what some people involved in service user groups said they wanted advisers to be – someone who:

listens carefully
guides but does not lead
helps when asked to
helps when we need it but not too much
should not boss you around
must have confidence in people
tries to understand how self-advocates feel
helps people to say what they feel
helps people to gain confidence in themselves.
(Wertheimer, 1988)

An experienced adviser said to us:

'Of primary importance is to have an understanding of the principles and values of self-advocacy. There's no blueprint. Different things help different groups. You start with "How do I do it without putting ideas in people's heads?" How do you do it if people haven't experienced responsibility before? You have to introduce people to the idea. It's a balancing act. It's quite tiring. When do you intervene or not? What risks do you allow? It's important for an adviser to have a support group, to meet your needs, to have someone else to talk to, someone you can trust, who will respect confidentiality. Some groups have two advisers.

Self-advocates want you to be a mixture of things: a friend, a teacher, sometimes a "parent", which I find quite hard. I want to act adult to adult. One Canadian adviser wonders if that happens more to women. Being an adviser is a continuing, evolving role, which you will discuss with people. You must have that dialogue. When people are trying to make decisions, it can be very difficult knowing when to intervene. I wait and wait before I intervene. I prefer that. If people are given enough time, they will usually resolve the problem. You mustn't impose your values and expectations on people. Someone in a group wants to send off letters that might be seen as outrageously demanding, couched in the wrong kind of terms. Some may feel it won't work, but people must be given the chance to do things in their own way. Sometimes when things have gone well or badly, I'll go home and write it all down. This kind of heartfelt stuff is difficult to put on

record, it's too personal; but it helps to look back on it, over time, to see how things have developed.'

Allies are workers and other people who support user and rights groups. This relationship can be a delicate one. There are still the risks for user groups of being taken over, patronised or exploited. But there are also the benefits of working with people who are on the inside, have special skills and access to resources. Many self-advocacy and self-help groups have gained much help from sympathetic professionals. But the relationship needs to be consistent with people's empowerment and on their *own* terms. This can be hard for groups who feel they are giving little back to people they value. It also demands a high degree of sensitivity on the part of allies. One moral might be 'choose your allies carefully'. A founder member of an organisation of disabled people said to us:

'We felt that we were often being taken over. When we were discussing what to do, the most helpful allies were among those who were keenest on having associate membership. They'd bring their skills and support, but wouldn't have a vote.'

A new paternalism?

Community development highlights some of the pressures inhibiting and undermining collective action. But it also points to a more general problem of participation. Instead of empowering us, efforts to involve people may have the *opposite* effect. Just imagine yourself appointed 'user rep' to a planning group, on your own, without experience, support or training. The result may be a new kind of paternalism – less visible, but no more emancipating than its predecessor.

A key cause of the problem is the competing need for involvement – but unequal balance of power – that generally exists between services and citizens. Their interests aren't necessarily the same. This is reflected in their different, sometimes conflicting philosophies of consumerism and empowerment. We may be starting to see a new and uneasy symbiotic relationship between service providers and users. Let's look at this more carefully.

Agencies and services have been under increasing pressure to 'listen to the voice of the consumer'. For some this has meant looking for legitimation from their users. Others are trying to involve them more actively and effectively. Either way, agencies are finding themselves needing their users in new ways. They want them to:

● run their own services
● comment on those they receive
● pass on information from their own experience.

But service users also need the agencies if they are to have more say. This is perhaps a paradox of empowerment. Groups still want something agencies have – their *power*. Trying to get it can leave them vulnerable and dependent. This brings us to the first of five expressions of this new paternalism we need to look at.

1. Manipulation

Agencies and organisations can play off and divide their users, ignore or incorporate them, pay lip service to their demands, or stonewall. We heard about one patients' council in a psychiatric hospital where, after initial support, managers stopped coming to meetings.

> **'In the early days, consultants thought it would fade away. Managers saw it as a way of getting power from them. Lack of management interest results in loss of user interest. You turn up sometimes and you feel a wally. Nothing happens. You wonder if there's something wrong with you. We need more support from managers.'**

There are experienced and highly skilled user groups that can take all this in their stride. Equally, there are others which are much more fragile, whose participants may already be under great stress. Their own need for some success to maintain their self-esteem and rally and recruit members can leave them even more exposed.

2. The marginalisation of participants

Participants can still find themselves marginalised. They may be invited on to public platforms, but essentially only to speak about themselves and their personal troubles. They aren't given the chance to participate in the process of converting these into public policy. That remains with the organising agencies. Issues of voyeurism and exploitation begin to surface. As a member of a service user group said in a meeting with a senior staff member of a large voluntary organisation,

> **'It's a bit upsetting if we're going to be asked to take part in your press conferences, but we're not being consulted on issues that concern us.'**

3. Taking over people's participation

Earlier we saw some of the difficulties of moving from professional to self-advocacy. There's another more subtle problem. Here it's not so much a matter of agencies opposing people's involvement as *taking it over*. The line between setting up user groups and colonising them can be a thin one. 'User-involvement' is already being staked out as another sphere for political, professional and research intervention. We've read articles by senior managers telling user groups what to do and how to organise. Conferences are organised on user participation and empowerment, but service users aren't necessarily involved in their planning.

Convincing arguments are offered for this. For example, people might not feel comfortable being involved. Should they be troubled? Who would you include and what about those you left out? We need professional as well as participatory forums. There are logistical problems. Tokenism must be avoided. All these arguments have a kernel of truth. But we can see how each may serve to maintain the status quo and keep the subjects of this debate at arm's length, just as they have been so often in the past. Welfare services seem to have an almost infinite capacity to undermine people's participation. In one project for young people, we saw how producing a newsletter could become as much an agency-imposed task as a means of self-expression.

4. Marginalising involvement

People want to get involved to change their lives but it can become a dead end instead. We have seen this in social services. 'User-run' services are set up, but the rest of the agency and people's relations with it stay the same. You can have a say in the running of the family centre, but no control in crucial dealings with social workers. Even the involvement that is offered may be qualified. People are still congregated and segregated instead of being accessed to mainstream opportunities. Take this self-run support group for mental health service users we visited.

It meets in a social services building. Some participants are described as 'volunteers'. There's a room for members of the users' committee. One member complains that they all segregate themselves in there. 'They want to be separate.' A community meeting is taking place. It's in a large room. It's modern but rather shabby. There are paintings on the walls by members as well as a lot of notices. There are some non-smoking times, but the air is thick with smoke. During part of the meeting, workers sit separately at a table, talking to each other. The major item on the agenda is subs. 'Some people don't pay.' 'It's a real problem.' It raises a lot of argument. 'We won't be able to afford to get in any more tea or coffee the way things are going.' 'We could charge for drinks instead.' 'That could really mount up for people on social security over a few days.' 'You'd have to check people paid.' One worker speaks firmly and at length and then leaves immediately. A lot of people sit without saying anything. There is a long desultory discussion. The issue is not resolved.

5. Involvement for agencies

People's involvement may primarily serve the agency's interests, not theirs. It can be used to manage people more closely, transfer responsibility to them, or obtain their information. For example, tenants are involved to reduce rent arrears and help run housing on inadequate budgets. We listened to one senior officer from a social work department talk glowingly of users meeting with council committee members so that they could see how satisfied people were and what useful work was being done. But would service users receive the same invitations to say what's *wrong* with services?

A checklist for change

If we are to prevent participatory initiatives falling into the same traps, we must constantly monitor them. Checklists for involvement can help agencies recognise and avoid them. For example:

● Whose idea was it?
Whose needs does it meet?
Who sets the agenda?
What does the agency want from involvement?
What do participants want from it?
Are the two clear to both?
What can people achieve by their involvement ?
Where can they get advice and support?
Whose forms and forums are used?
Who controls them?
Who actually gets involved?
Who writes the accounts?
Who controls information and decides what to do with it?
● Who plans events like workshops and conferences?

In this chapter we've seen some of the difficulties associated with community development and ways in which agencies can take people over. Next we shall look at how people can get together to gain more say for themselves.

7

Guidelines for Involvement: Empowering Ourselves

We shouldn't be surprised that an idea as radical and far-reaching as empowerment attracts so many myths and legends. Some commentators make it appear almost impossible. Others skate over the difficulties so it seems easy. Neither is true. Neither is likely to be helpful. The two of us have seen many shining examples of people gaining more say over their lives and services. We have also seen initiatives which seem to *over*power rather than empower people. If anything demands rigour rather than rhetoric, it's empowerment. Let's begin with two examples that more than make the point. First a user group.

The meeting is in a large double room in a social services drop-in centre. There are three paintings on the wall, six copies of a play on an old wooden cupboard, a cigarette-stained carpet and institutional chairs. Another pile of hard chairs are stacked against a wall. Fourteen people sit round. The light is switched on in their half of the room, the neon for the other is off, leaving it dark and drab. Half the people are smoking. An extractor fan rattles, but makes little impact. The community worker has made a pot of tea. Only a few people take up her offer to get themselves a cup. Discussion begins.

Anne: **I was in hospital with depression. Not once did anyone ask me why I was depressed, particularly at that time.**

128

You weren't invited to talk about your own problems. What I'd gone in for was some enlightenment.

Dave: We've set up a new group. We are very assertive people. We know how to put pressure. Our group's for people to be able to participate in their own welfare. We will decide what we are going to do and how to do it.

Mary: It could be another splinter group.

Dave: Yes, but we feel we have got our own character and we have to develop that first. I've just heard this week that we are being recognised from very high.

Joan: There's so many little groups everywhere that nothing, well very little gets through. _

Anne: You find yourself totally dependent on someone to help you, to find out. It's taken me three years to find out about therapy, gestalt . . . and now it's too late.

Dave from the new group dominates the meeting. Most exchanges are two-way, between him and someone else. Less than half the people present say anything. There seem to be many different agendas, around both personal and group issues. Dave is clear: 'The Director is very interested in us. We had a group of patients come to see us, to see what they want. The points that I put to them were these . . .' John on the other hand is uncertain. 'I got on to this committee. Suddenly I was very powerful. I was talking to important people. I was on the local executive committee. I wondered whose opinions I was offering, who I was representing. I resigned, but I did have a lot of influence then.'

Next is a day conference about disabled people speaking for themselves organised by a group of disabled people.

One hundred and fifty people sit in a vast cold council chamber. A series of six speakers, with opening remarks from the two people chairing sessions, has been organised for the morning. The very full agenda overruns as it takes people much longer than expected to book in and then get their mid-morning coffee. At the end of the morning the programme offers the opportunity for 'questions from participants'. 'Why can we only ask questions and the platform make statements?' demands someone from the floor. The public address system isn't working properly. People with hearing disabilities shout that they cannot hear. 'Blame the electricians, not me', says the chair.

At lunchtime it takes Ken, who has cerebral palsy, 15 minutes to walk the long corridor to get his meal. 'They asked me if I wanted a wheelchair when I got here. No way am I going to do that.'

One part of the afternoon is set aside for small workshops. There are about 15 people in each. People introduce themselves and offer their agendas. 'I am the workshop leader, but I will not be leading you.' Each person speaks through the leader and some put up their hands to speak. Some people know each other, others don't. There is a sense of pressure to come up with proposals to influence the direction the conference takes; 75 minutes hardly seems enough time.

Of course not every effort to get involved and take control is like this. But all face the same kind of difficulties. These examples highlight three important issues. First, we must take active steps to make possible people's empowerment. It doesn't just come naturally. It's no more likely to follow from the earnest desire of service users than from agencies having their hearts in the right place. Second, it's not just service providers who make mistakes trying to involve people. All of us can do it badly. Finally, gaining more say may not just mean learning new lessons but *unlearning* old ones. The conference organisers seemed to rely on traditional political and trade union forms and structures they were used to. This certainly didn't help to empower participants.

A process of empowerment

There is no ready-made model of empowerment and it would probably be a mistake to look for one. But there is one thing that existing experience does suggest. Empowerment doesn't follow from a set of rules or procedures. It is a *process*. This process enables us to make the connection between our private troubles and public policy. It makes possible the journey from our own personal needs to influencing and changing attitudes, values, policy and practice that affect them. It has several constituents. They aren't separate steps or stages, but overlapping elements. They include:

● developing our own accounts
● forming our own judgements
● negotiating with others.

They raise other issues and there are other dimensions to explore, but let's begin with these.

Developing our own accounts

This is the starting point for our empowerment. It means putting together our views, our versions of things. We begin by articulating our wants and experience. Once we put our individual accounts together, we become aware of the similarities and overlaps with other people's. We discover there's nothing strange or special about us. *It isn't just me.* I'm not the only woman who feels lonely stuck at home with a young baby. Other people have the same problems living on income support. Our thoughts and ideas aren't just moans, grumbles and gossip. They aren't merely anecdotal or apocryphal. They don't have to be hidden, secret and illegitimate. They are helpful and important. We have a right to express them. We begin to see that they have validity alongside other more powerful accounts. We have our side of the story to tell too.

We may not have formulated our ideas or put them into words before. They may have been confined to individual thoughts, private conversations or informal discussions. Something happens to change this. The trigger may be a chance remark or meeting, something we read, someone actually asking us, wanting to get something done, or desperation. For many people it's a giant step. It may take great courage. But it's also liberating. This is what one single parent claimant who got involved in a campaigning group said:

**'Things really started when we told each other our stories.
Not in so many words, but that's what it boiled down to.
They'd gone through things just like me. We had a good
laugh about some of it. It made me feel much better. It put it
in a different light.'**

Developing our own accounts helps us to realise that we really
can speak for ourselves. It's both part of the process of
empowerment and a strategy to achieve it. It may be
informal – just talking to each other, or become much
more, generating our own media, using some of the forms
we described earlier, like newsletters and videos. It may lead
us to mainstream print and broadcast media; to access
programmes and magazines on news stands.

Forming our own judgements

It's one thing to talk about our feelings and experience. It can
be quite another to work out what changes we'd like to see
and how to bring them about. It's this process of forming our
own judgements we come to next. We may not have much
experience of it. Years of exclusion can leave people feeling
it's something they can't do. When they are invited to get
involved, as we have seen, it may only be to talk about their
personal trials and tribulations. Earlier we referred to one
consultation about council services which showed the similarities between the views of active feminists and other women.
One difference that did emerge was that most women were
not used to formulating their ideas in terms of demands.
Statements like 'I want' or 'we need' 'were not heard
frequently' (Kettleborough, 1988).
    Agencies seeking people's involvement often forget this.
They expect them to come up quickly with ideas and
proposals without any real chance to think them through.
But it is through a process of discussion, learning and
cooperation that we can begin to **agree agendas**, **develop
demands** and **make decisions**. This process involves both
personal and group development, in close interaction. We

begin with our personal experiences and agendas, which may be vague and unformulated. As we exchange our individual accounts, we build a shared perspective. Ideas develop and attitudes change. Personal opinions inform and give rise to collective views. Personal positions and needs grow into group judgements.

We work out what we think. We find out where we agree and disagree. Then we can decide what we want to do together. By framing such discussions initially in terms of our own wants and circumstances instead of services to meet them, our thinking isn't constrained by the limitations of those we know. We find out more about what might be possible as we go on. All this requires time and reflection. We need all the elements we talked about earlier, like information, support and confidence-building. Let's listen again to the single parent claimant.

> 'After we'd met several times we all began to get a bit of a feel for it. We talked about what we could do. Somebody would come up with an idea. We'd talk about it. Some wouldn't be any use, but there were one or two really good ones. I felt much better. Before I'd felt really embarrassed. I'd thought I can't do this. What am I doing here? And I think the others felt the same. This didn't stop us arguing about how we were going to do something. But in the end we split into groups and each group worked on a different idea. It depended on what people wanted to do.'

A meeting bringing together disabled people, people with learning difficulties and people with mental distress to strengthen alliances between them, used a helpful agenda:

● Who are we and what do we want?
● What have we found that works?
● What can help?
● What can we do together?

Once we have reached this stage, we are in a position to work out what methods and approaches to use to gain more say.

This could include taking a place on a consultative committee, using legislation, publishing a research report or taking direct action. We can weigh up the pros and cons of each and decide what combination to use them in. We can identify any problems they pose. What kind of demonstration will gain rather than alienate public support? How do we get media coverage which doesn't perpetuate negative stereotypes?

By now we're likely to have a better idea of how to find things out and a clearer picture of the world we are working in. This chapter rests on that belief. The aim is not to take readers through an endless list of tactics and techniques for empowerment – this is how you lobby members of parliament or get money from your local council – but to explore the process we must all go through to be able to make our *own* choices and develop our own forms for empowerment.

Negotiating with others

An old argument against involving people is that they won't agree about anything. 'How can you have community involvement when there's no such thing as a community view?' But participation doesn't assume consensus. It is concerned with the *negotiation of conflict*. Excluding people only makes conflict worse. Being involved makes it possible to work through our differences. Negotiation is central to people's empowerment. As one young man with learning difficulties said:

> **'The MPs should talk to us before they make any more decisions. We're the people they should negotiate with.'**

First, as we have seen, we negotiate with each other. Then when we have worked out what we want, we negotiate with other interests and organisations to achieve it. It's a continuing process of dialogue and exchange. It begins with recognition of the validity of our own *and* other people's perspectives. It's not just service users and providers who have different, sometimes competing interests, but also service users and other citizens and direct and indirect service users, like disabled people and carers and people with mental distress and their families. Without negotiation, our positions are likely to become polarised. In Britain, for instance, the national organisation for people with mental distress has argued for the closure of psychiatric hospitals while that for their relatives has pressed to keep them. Both have now set up their own 'user groups'.

Negotiation requires personal and group skills and resources. It doesn't always work and it may not be easy. Sometimes people won't want to negotiate. It's as likely to entail hard talking as constructive conversation. But it can prevent and resolve problems. It means that people are part of the discussion and their voice can be heard. A number of people have emphasised its importance to us. For instance, this adult education teacher and trainer working with people who have learning difficulties and staff to support self-advocacy, said:

> 'The latest video we have made is a trigger for discussion. I feel it's important for people to sit and hear each other, to enable people to come together and go away and work together. I feel my job is to talk with people and workers and then bring them together – to give them permission to talk together.'

And a consultant working with parents of disabled children:

> 'My role is to help families and workers to renegotiate among themselves and with each other what's best to do. Families have little information. Services are defensive.'

It's not easy and it begs some difficult questions. One campaigner, after reading the first draft of this book, wrote to us:

> 'What happens if there are deep differences of opinion or conflicts of interest between different citizens or groups of citizens? Who is to be the arbiter? Does it fall back on the agency concerned? If so on what basis does the agency decide – the majority view? But that could mean that the interests of the most powerless minority groups were overridden. If

opinions and interests are fairly evenly divided, how then? Isn't there a danger that an agency could use such divisions to go ahead with whatever they wanted to do in the first place and they could say, quite legitimately, that they had acted on the basis of their consultations?'

She raised some difficult questions and, as she said, there is no easy answer. But her comments again highlight the importance of:

● providing support for people's involvement so that it can be broad-based
● ensuring there is time and opportunity for negotiation
● agencies not using the difficulties people encounter in agreeing agendas and action as an opportunity to continue to impose their own
● developing ways of empowering ourselves which challenge rather than reflect the broader exclusions and discriminations of society.

Learning to work together

Central to this process of empowerment is being able to work together. It's easily forgotten, until things go wrong. Take some of the issues people have raised with us. What do you do about the person who always wants to talk about their personal problems? What about *hidden* power and agendas? How do we stop ourselves giving more weight to one person's views than to another's, or deal with someone who seems to be pursuing their own plans regardless of the rest of us? People have offered some helpful guidelines. 'Try and make issues explicit.' 'Help others speak by making room for them.' But this isn't just a matter of techniques or personalities. How successfully we deal with these difficulties depends on how well we learn to work together. This isn't something that just happens. We have to work at it, using the kinds of forms and forums that encourage openness and exchange. The sorts of skills and relationships involved may be quite different from those we're used to at home or at work.

Listening is an important part of the process of learning to work together. We may hear things which we don't at first understand, don't like, or find uncomfortable. We don't have to agree with what other people say, but we will learn a lot and understand them better if we try and listen to them. Listening to others is the other half of speaking for ourselves.

Skilled support can help. We have already seen how useful advisers can be. When one of us was involved in a claimants' group, we enlisted the aid of a consultant. She helped us work out what we wanted to do and discover with whom we could and couldn't work.

Getting to know each other is also important if we are to develop trust, confidence and understanding. One thing that has struck us about many successful user and rights groups is the closeness of their members' relationships with each other. As a member of one said, 'You need to be able to share your feelings with others.' Early on, one member of the claimants' group had the idea of meeting in someone's house one evening with some refreshments. Everyone came. We talked to each other. It worked. It was much more pleasant after that. Fostering our relationships is an important part of working together for empowerment.

'Difficult people'. Agencies can be quick to dismiss people who want more say as difficult and self-seeking. If they think people's egos are over-large, they should ask themselves whether they make it possible for any but the most determined to have a say. But there are also implications here for initiatives for empowerment. People who have been denied a say are often desperate to have one. Sometimes people have been damaged by the welfare services they are trying to challenge. They may find it difficult to be reasonable after years of being devalued and disempowered. This can then make it hard for others to have *their* say. This is an issue that can't just be sidestepped or glossed over. User groups should recognise and learn to deal with it. One adviser said, 'There is a role here to support people, but not to pathologise them.' Working with each other won't always be a comfortable ride.

Enabling newcomer involvement

If the initial difficulty for a group is how to get together, gain confidence and skills and work effectively together, the second is how to *stay open to new involvement*. We have already seen some of the obstacles to people's involvement. It's not the norm. Most of us don't expect to have a say. There are many negative stereotypes for people who do, like 'they're all extremists' and 'it's politically motivated'. It may mean 'coming out' and being associated with a stigmatised identity. We shall be hearing a lot in this chapter from organisations of disabled people. They've made some of the greatest progress towards empowerment. Listen to what one said about involving people:

> **'A lot don't want to get involved in campaigning. A mystique is attached to it. There's some feeling that if you rock the boat they'll take away what you've got. They want to get on living.'**

It's important for empowering groups and organisations to be sensitive to this if they are to move beyond the same small circle of faces and involve previously unaffiliated people. But there are some real tensions here. Once we get to know each other and work well, it's tempting to keep things as they are. We have caught ourselves thinking like this; reluctant to risk the progress we have made and really only wanting more people like us! Then what we may see as our hard-won solidarity can easily feel like a clique to outsiders. How do we stop ourselves becoming yet another barrier to other people's involvement and empowerment?

The answer seems to be for groups to see involvement as a continuing process of accessing newcomers, sharing skills and sharing power. One community group we came across had a policy of apprenticing new members, supporting them to try different tasks, from chairing meetings and appearing on television to meeting with council officials. But this may be more easily said than done for many hard-pressed groups. For instance:

'We probably don't do enough to get a wide range of people involved. We need to do a lot of contacting and discussing with disabled people in the borough. It's not enough just to have a representative on our committee. Whatever we may think of it, users of a day centre may not want it to close. It's important to have a dialogue with them. It's important to be in touch with the grass roots. That is an important skill. We have been accused of being "articulate". But we aren't able to get out to day centres as we'd like to. Our resources are limited. We have three and a bit paid staff and their time is mostly office based. Over the past years we have gone out to some groups to talk about what we do. But we rely on members of our management committee going back to their groups and telling them.'

It's also important to remember that when people get involved they have different degrees of experience and understanding. What may be old hat for one may be totally unknown to another. It's no use expecting newcomers to take your experience on trust. When we heard one member of an organisation of disabled people tell others, 'Don't do this. I've made many mistakes along these lines', the reaction was anger not acceptance. People want to find out for *themselves*. Just because we have worked through our values and principles doesn't mean these don't have to be constantly renegotiated, if others are to feel they own them too. As we shall see shortly, where this doesn't happen, it's very easy for agencies and authorities to divide and rule.

Enabling broad-based involvement

Enabling broad-based involvement is as important as accessing newcomers. If our efforts to empower ourselves don't extend to all groups, then they are only likely to perpetuate the existing dominance of white, middle-class, conventionally articulate people. There's no reason to assume that rights and user groups are less discriminatory than anyone else. Some groups, for example, are predominantly white. Members of minority ethnic groups may want to organise separately. But that's no reason for not facilitating their involvement elsewhere. It's not enough to send out mailings and minutes to black organisations, or conclude that there's little indication they want to be involved if they don't reply to written invitations. The essential lesson here seems to be to go out to people, rather than expect them to come to you. This is what the editorial group of a newspaper for older people did. They already had a wide racial mix, including Afro-Caribbeans, Jews and someone who was Turkish.

> **'We're very anxious that the paper should reach more ethnic minority people and we should have Asian people on the editorial group. We couldn't get the whole newspaper translated. We used to have translations on the back page. That didn't reach people. For example we couldn't get appropriate dialects of the different Asian languages and we had Hebrew rather than Yiddish. So for this issue we've just done, we went to visit an Asian day centre and interviewed and photographed people there rather than having a translation. This has been very successful and we want to do this kind of thing again. We hope that this way we'll get to talk to more Asian people and ask them to be involved.'**

Take the experience of an organisation of disabled people.

> **'We've done a lot of work with limited success. We work with some individual families. We don't have the same number of black and Asian people seeking information – very few. We've done the normal things, leaflets, posters in minority languages, but we haven't interpreting. There aren't any organisations of black disabled people in this borough. We want to take a pro-active stance. Recently we've been having more talks with black and Asian groups. We've been told by black and Asian colleagues in other areas that we need to employ a black and Asian worker. We've tried to get money for one.'**

This raises another key issue – resources. Empowerment still has low priority for funding. The only offices groups can afford may have restricted physical access. They may not have enough workers to broaden their base. There's no money for interpreting or translating information. These costs must be recognised and funders who are serious about empowerment should be prepared to pay them.

Three issues for empowerment

Developing our knowledge

Whether or not knowledge is power, we certainly need it to empower ourselves. The newsletters and bulletins user groups produce keep people in touch, provide support, develop discussion and generate information. An educationalist working in a centre in the United States providing training for and by community activists identified three sources of knowledge for empowerment:

● regaining information from experts
● regaining our own knowledge
● creating new knowledge.

'It's teaching people how to reclaim the knowledge extracted from them, the intellectual capital ripped off them, for example learning to read the medical records of toxin-poisoned children. Recouping people's own knowledge through oral history. Helping people make their own surveys, doing the research that professionals won't do. Bringing people together, sharing struggles, transcribing and then getting a subgroup to choose lessons they feel important to share, so they publish what they want.'

Sharing skills

People seeking a say mostly learn informally, from each other and through experience. But there's also a place for other opportunities for learning. Let's hear again from the American educationalist:

'You work with small groups and then they go out and spread what they have learned. People involved in common struggle, teaching each other. It's very important that people don't come alone but in twos and threes, reporting back, accountable to their project. It avoids creating leaders. Workshops are generally a weekend and then come again, not just once. It's important you work with people over a period.'

A college offering access courses for local people emphasised the importance of putting people at ease:

'The vast majority of students are nervous at the thought of staying in a formal educational setting. The students and children are made welcome. Meals are inviting. If social events are friendly, then the ice will be broken. If we can overcome fears and worries there is ample evidence that students can achieve major breakthroughs in confidence and learning. If these issues are not overcome, it is likely that students will remember the course as a time of loneliness, frustration and humiliation.'

Working with professionals

We all need experts and professionals sometimes, not just for support or as allies, but for their skills. These can be difficult relationships. You may discover you can do it better yourself, like the community group we were involved in, whose members realised they could represent themselves more effectively at planning public inquiries than highly paid lawyers could. We could often say what we wanted more accurately. They couldn't invest as much time and commitment. We weren't imprisoned by the same assumptions about how we ought to behave and what was and wasn't possible. You may want experts to show you how to do something, or keep control over what they are doing. As one trainer said:

'It's about making a video or whatever. You have to develop contracts with professionals. Avoid the hired gun syndrome.

Instead say: "You don't make a decision without us having a meeting between us. We have a say in the decision."'

Forums for empowerment

We may seek empowerment by setting up our own organisations and forums. We may turn to other people's. Some of us will do both. There's an important distinction to draw between **agency-** or **service-provider**-led initiatives for involvement and **citizen**-led ones. The first tend to focus on involving people in participatory structures and service systems. The second are more clearly concerned with increasing people's control over their lives. Each has its advantages and disadvantages. We control our own forums. We can agree their agenda and structure. The main problem may be getting money and other resources. Agency forums have mushroomed in Britain. Their strength is that they can give people access, credibility and the chance to change organisations from within. Their shortcoming may be that people have little control over their structure, the conditions of their involvement or how much say they have. It's not always clear whether they are offering involvement in decision-making or merely consultation. Usually it's only the latter. They also pose problems of co-option and incorporation.

Some people are reluctant to get sucked into agency structures. One woman said to us, 'Why should people want to get involved in their power-hungry organisations?' A health services manager said: 'If you cover all the options for supporting people to take part in formal participatory arrangements, like the place, timing, expenses, conditions, etc., and they still don't get involved, then perhaps the reservations you have always had about those structures are true.' A member of a group of recipients of mental health services asked:

'Do these arrangements just syphon us off from more appropriate activities? We're concerned with how our lives can be improved. Should we be getting involved in services at

all? In many cases they are the wrong kind of response to our needs.'

The answer to his second question may depend on whether services are *mainstream* or *segregating* ones. But if we want to get involved in wider debates and influence attitudes, policy and practice, it's very difficult to ignore agency-led initiatives for involvement. For good or ill, they are an important feature on the landscape. A worker with an organisation of disabled people said:

'We never leave conferences altogether, however bad. We'll try and get some kind of makeshift leaflet done or talk to people. People on the platform may be the only ones who don't agree with you.'

But as he went on to say:

'You could spend the whole time reacting to initiatives you didn't like and not get your own things done.'

People seeking more say have to strike a balance between **initiating** their own activities and **responding** to other people's. It's difficult because outcomes are often unpredictable. You just don't know when something is going to work and when it's a waste of time. The lesson seems to be to put most emphasis on your own concerns and forums and learn how to deal with other people's. Here's what the young woman who was co-opted on to a council subcommittee had to say about that.

'I think it was even more difficult for me because I was in care in that borough. When I first met the area manager at the committee I was frightened. It was the same one as when I was in care. I don't have that feeling anymore – that they know everything about me. Looking back on it, I know things about them. Skills you need? You need to speak the jargon, or a certain amount of it. You mustn't get angry. It goes against people like me. Councillors get angry. The one time I did, everybody turned on me.

You need to know the game, otherwise you're lost. You'd forever be saying things in the meeting and not knowing if they're listening. You have to know where the power is. You work it out from the structure. Who is responsible for what – councillors and officers. Being in care, being involved in user groups, going to college, all help. You need to know what you can do, what rights you have as a co-opted member. Whether you can vote, whether you can write to officers and members. You can go on relevant training courses. I went on a study day about secure accommodation. Black people are over-represented in secure accommodation.'

Starting with our own forums

Getting involved in other people's forums can be a harsh and unpleasant business. This experience one of us had brings into sharp relief some more general problems. It was a European tribunal set up by a women's organisation to give poor women a chance to give testimony and develop demands. Poor women were grateful for a chance to speak. 'This is the first time I have ever left Italy, ever been on a plane,' one said. But it was still the organisers who made the crucial decisions. They decided the agenda, shaped the procedure and chose who would give testimony. At the press conference, they faced the media while the participants sat behind it. One woman had a panic attack after she gave her testimony. Another felt she would never have been chosen because her story was 'not dramatic enough'.

We were told that we should work out our demands. But there wasn't time to formulate them properly. We weren't given the chance to report back from workshops ourselves. At the end of one, an organiser gave us five demands to vote on. One woman said she couldn't see how they had managed to come up with a series of demands by the end of the tribunal. 'Where had they come from?'

But women weren't able to deal with these difficulties. British delegates weren't staying together and with a packed programme, there were few opportunities to talk or get to know each other. German women left early. We were never able to have our own meetings with interpreters, but without the organisers. We weren't able to sort out our feelings or work out what to do. Some women were upset and disappointed. Others didn't seem to know what was happening.

Most of us don't like to create conflict. We begin to feel like a nuisance and our self-doubts grow. Are we going over the top? Have we been unfair? Aren't they doing the best they can?

Members of disability, user and rights groups emphasise two key ways of dealing with these difficulties: assertiveness skills and support from each other. Self-assertion helps us to cope with frustrations and failures as well as achieve successes. Our own organisations provide support. They validate our experience. We no longer have to take things personally. For instance:

> **'It's the collectivity of disabled people that makes it easier for me personally and politically to sustain criticisms and attacks.'**

> **'We've all learnt, some with short sharp shocks. You get it through experience and with the confidence of having the organisation behind you. You are the representative of an organisation of disabled people.'**

The crucial point seems to be to **start with your own forums** before getting involved in anyone else's. The tribunal was an example of what can happen when isolated and inexperienced individuals seek empowerment through other people's arrangements. As an activist involved in the disability movement said:

> **'The movement has a history, networks. We report back. We develop discussion and ideas through that. We are part of that. Things develop from that. Nothing is in isolation.'**

Professionals have time and opportunities to develop their skills and agendas. If we are to take part in their conferences, write in their publications or sit on their committees, we must first develop our own organisations and forums. These can offer us the skills and solidarity we need to enter someone else's. First we get together in our own groups, then we can negotiate with theirs. This also offer us the option of negotiating *directly* with other agencies and interests as well as through specific participatory structures.

Building empowering forums

We have seen people in agency-led forums intimidated by rudeness, anger and procedures, and silenced by their own politeness. But people seeking more say should look as critically at their own forums as at other people's. It's important that these don't just duplicate their deficiencies. They must deal with the same issues of access, equal opportunities, language and information, usually without enough time or resources.

Citizen involvement is an international movement. Its forums range from small local groups to international organisations. In Britain, for example, local groups of disabled people come together in umbrella organisations. There is a national organisation of disabled people managed by representatives of national and local disabled people's organisations and an international organisation governed by national representatives. Such structures run the same risk as any others of becoming distant and losing touch. The crucial lesson that has been learned is to build them from the bottom, rooted in local memberships, and to be ever aware of these dangers.

Informal structures for involvement seem to be the most attractive and effective. But there is pressure to formalise them to ensure representation, accountability and funding. It's a tension that may be difficult to resolve. An adviser of an organisation of young people in care told us:

> 'Even the vocabulary changed when we got the grant. Instead of "young people", "children" slipped out occasionally. Either you get the money and it's changed or you don't and die. We had fluctuating groups, we had weekends, social things, a band, young people expressing themselves, confidence, jokes. Not just an on-going membership thing. Fun and enjoyment were central.

That's missing in a bureaucratic environment. We tapped in on it in the past. It's got to be re-created. All that went when we had full-timers. We were losing the grassroots. The dilemma of full-time and grassroots. The worker role was meant to be developing membership but actually became involved in raising the profile and general issues. We had minutes. We were bureaucratised. But you've got to have some of that. There are a lot of issues that need to be addressed at national level, so you can't just be local. How to deal with it? Start from local networks, not from the top. Accept things should come and go.'

Pressures against empowerment

Rights and service users' organisations report other pressures from agencies and authorities. As people with learning difficulties soon discovered, they want **leaders**.

'They try and create leaders. In the United States people said "Beware the superstar syndrome." People feel pressures on them to be a leader – to hold it all together. You have to learn to say no.'

They want people to speak with a **single voice**. This is what the secretary of a national organisation of people with mental distress said:

'Organisations are happy to set you up as the voice of users, so that they can then just relate to you. They speak to you and say they have consulted with users. The same is true with the media that want an easily reached port of call to get the other point of view.'

This might meet their needs by making self-advocacy more like them. But it hardly accords with its goal of enabling people to *speak for themselves*.

'We aren't all the same. The only thing we may have in common is the mistreatment we may share through use of some service or the attachment of some stigmatic label. All of us aren't equal as service users. The wider discriminations still apply. We have to recognise this and try to find ways of overcoming it in how we work together. Neither we nor service providers should assume consensus among us. There isn't a "users' view". It won't help to try and impose one on people. We will have different political and personal opinions. People's experience of services may lead them to some common views about the political problems that underlie it, but even that shouldn't be taken for granted. We're not a pressure group. This isn't a single issue campaign. We're an organisation campaigning for people to be able to speak for themselves.'

The search for charismatic leaders and 'the user view' can be damaging and divisive. It can be very tempting for vulnerable organisations and people who have long been denied a say. But agencies are then among the first to accuse them both of being *unrepresentative*.

Representation

Self-advocacy organisations face a double difficulty. First, they have all the problems, but usually few of the resources to involve people as widely as they want. Second, they can expect to be dismissed as unrepresentative. 'Who gave you a mandate?' 'Who are you accountable to?' Once they raise issues of wide concern to their constituency and become involved in representative structures, they can expect the same objections as women's and ethnic minority organisations before them. But no organisation can ever include everyone or reflect every perspective. Self-advocacy organisations are subject to the same limitations as others, no more, no less. Community and user groups have long been aware of the importance of formal representation. They are democratically constituted organisations. Their representatives are elected. They have opposed the co-option and election to participatory structures of unaffiliated individuals.

Instead of using representation as an excuse to exclude people, agencies and authorities should first examine their *own* arrangements for involvement. Are they providing the necessary **access** and **support** for people to make possible broad-based involvement in their organisation? People's reluctance to get involved has much to do with the difficulties of doing so. Representation raises complex issues of political philosophy. But the whole point of empowerment is *speaking for ourselves*. Members of user and rights groups rarely claim to speak for other people. Their main demand is for people to have more say. As one disabled man said:

> **'If you are a representative it's important that you are clear who you are representing and to whom you are accountable, and that the agency knows and agrees this. Your validity may be your experience, for example of disability, or of using a particular service. You speak for yourself. No, you can't represent all disabled people, but you can speak from your experience and perhaps represent a specific group.'**

One campaigner made a broader point:

> **'We have the tradition of involvement through the representative democratic processes of the town hall. Doesn't the need for other involvement opportunities imply that these processes have failed? And if new models of participation rely – as they often do – on representation, aren't they subject to the same weaknesses, *and also* democratically suspect because they are based on inadequately defined constituencies?'**

What we may be seeing is a clash between the very different cultures of empowerment and traditional management and political structures. The 'representativeness' of rights and service user organisations shouldn't be made the scapegoat for the much bigger issues they raise. Instead the much more difficult task that may face us all is to find new approaches for citizen involvement.

Who are we?

Rights and service user groups have to grapple with issues of identity as well as representation. As we have suggested, it's not always helpful to think of 'service users' as a separate group. Sometimes though, people may want to emphasise their differences, if only to avoid the intrusion of outsiders, particularly service providers. We have seen the argument 'we're all service users really', used by service providers to try and straddle the fence and marginalise people on the receiving end of the most stigmatising services. Disabled people have had to contend with the argument 'everyone's disabled in some way' to deny the particular oppression they face. So long as people have to unite to deal with discrimination and difficult services, there is likely to be a need for separate identities. But 'users' too, are not always sure who they are. As a member of a group of recipients of psychiatric services said:

'Every time we have a discussion about our constitution, the question of what is a "user" crops up. Is it just that you've been to your doctor, or you've been prescribed tranquillizers, or that you've been a hospital patient? Some people feel you've got to have been in hospital to be a user.'

Then there is the question of when are you a 'user' and when an 'ex-user'. Exploring these issues, one woman has written of the permanent effects, both practical and psychological, she feels her experience of psychiatric services has had for her.

'Will a flood of imposters claim free membership? . . . I cannot imagine many people claiming to be service users if it is not true. If a person wishes to be defined as a psychiatric service user or ex-user then that is good enough for me.'

As with other labels, it is perhaps what people directly affected *themselves* have to say that should finally guide us.

It's also important to consider which is our *defining* identity. A local authority disability training officer who was himself disabled talked about his potentially conflicting roles.

> '**I am an officer. I'm not a representative of disabled people. I'm not elected by organisations of disabled people. Users of the day centre have now got me off the committee. They said: "We don't want to be seen as your puppet." I could see what they meant.**'

Running our own services

Although, as we have emphasised, it's not the only one, a key objective of empowerment is having a say in the services we use. There are different ways of doing this. One is to **offer each other services**. Peer counselling provided by disabled people and co-counselling where two people give each other equal time as client and counsellor are examples of this. So are self-help and mutual aid projects. People's shared experience becomes a strength instead of being seen as a problem. This self-help project for people with AIDS offers individual advice, support and grants:

> '**We do have an understanding amongst each other. There's an empathy rather than a sympathy. We all want sympathy when first diagnosed with AIDS but we also want some empathy . . . If you're talking with someone with empathy you often get more constructive answers. Because we have similar experiences, there can be an equality between us . . . It's about working with someone, not *for* them. We don't dump stuff on people. We don't just come in. People choose to come to us.**'

Alternatively, people may **run their own personal services**. Here individualised funding is made directly available to a person or in some cases a trust is set up in their name. In this way disabled people have established their own self-operated support schemes, designing their own support proposal and then employing their own support staff.

The problem that can arise with a simple purchase of service model – 'give us the money so we can choose what we want' – is that it may still leave people dependent on what service providers are prepared to offer and what accords with the dictates of the market.

A third option is for people to **set up and run their own services**. A black analyst identified the dilemma for members of minority ethnic groups of mainstream services which neither provide the services they want, nor resource people properly to provide them themselves.

> **'Where the community sets up alternatives, control stays with the mainstream in an inhibiting way. Short term funding, no security. Black organisations arising and then failing. They're set up to fail. They're offered no organisational support. Local authorities feeling "We can't do it. You understand your people. Go and do it." Ethnic minority service providers are in unequal relation. They are very much at grass roots level. Black churches have set up their own services.'**

Just offering our own services may make little mark on mainstream provision and leave us marginalised. It can mean we have *more* responsibility but no more power. Workers of a coalition of disabled people said:

> **'We have discussed providing services on our own terms . . . People like us feel we've got to become service providers because of political pressure. A lot of voluntary organisations are increasingly under that pressure and the reasons for coming into being can get lost.'**

What may be needed is a **twofold approach**, working for change in existing services as well as providing our own. This is what one man involved in the disabled people's movement said:

> **'We live in a world where there are service infrastructures, so we must ask how we can shape and adapt those services to meet our needs rather than them expect you to provide your own services. The question is how can we collaborate and cooperate so we can retain control of what happens to us and**

have access to their resources. We've got to look at the relation between our services and changing and controlling mainstream services. You need a compromise, services provided by social services with the influence of disabled people. The crucial problem is that the structure of social services will have to change to facilitate changes in services. I feel it can from experience we already have.'

We visited a centre for integrated living which has tried to do just this, 'working in a participative manner with service agencies to effect change', using a framework for the development of services based on 'the seven needs' disabled people have identified – information, counselling, housing, aids, personal help, transport and access (Wood, 1988).

Once we run our own services, we must beware of replacing one overpowering relationship with another by *disempowering* the people who now work for us. After years at the mercy of professionals, disabled people have demanded choice and control of personal helpers. We talked to a volunteer working with a disabled person who said she had few clear rights in the relationship. 'At present it's a matter of relying on the reasonableness of the person you are working with.' A care attendants scheme provided by an organisation of disabled people tried to address this.

'The scheme provides detailed guidelines to care attendants and users of the scheme; what you can and can't expect from it. Both are given confidential assessment forms at the end and care attendants know that at any time they can contact coordinators if they are unsure or unhappy about what they are doing or being asked to do. It's a service that meets needs and isn't oppressive.'

Guidelines for empowerment

We can summarise the issues we have discussed in this chapter in a brief set of guidelines and principles for people's empowerment.

Empowerment is a process which entails:

> developing our own accounts
> forming our own judgements
> negotiating with others.

To help us do this we need to:

> learn to work together
> enable newcomer and broad-based involvement
> start with our own forums and organisations before getting involved in other people's
> ensure our forums and organisations do not reflect prevailing exclusions and discriminations
> speak for ourselves, not other people
> resist outside pressures towards disempowering processes.

Schemes for citizen involvement we have been in touch with also emphasise the importance of:

> monitoring the costs and gains of taking part in agency-led initiatives for involvement to check whether it's worthwhile
> recognising the tensions between formal and informal arrangements for empowerment
> being honest about any problems encountered so that others can learn from them
> identifying examples of good practice to develop benchmarks of what's possible
> starting locally, but working at all levels: local, national and international
> identifying key allies and supporters who will help but not take over
> developing regular exchanges to draw together the lessons and experience gained by different groups in different spheres
> gaining a realistic appreciation of the obstacles in the way of empowerment without being inhibited by them

Now let's look at how agencies and their workers can meet people seeking a say half-way by developing their own empowering practice.

8

Guidelines for Involvement: Developing an Empowering Practice as Workers

Empowerment is a critical concept for practice. It puts power centre stage, reminding us that agencies and their workers can take power from people, but also have a part to play in helping them regain it. Of course, we need to be helped rather than hindered and supported rather than squashed whatever kind of agency or service we turn to, from town planning to car repairs. But empowerment has special reverberations for services like health and welfare because they intervene intimately in our lives, are meant to help and can restrict our rights.

First a word of warning. Workers do not operate in isolation. The role and nature of the organisations they work for affect what they can do. They also play a part in defining their relationship with other citizens. Developing a sensitive and empowering practice may be at the heart of their agency's objectives. Alternatively, it may be something they work towards almost *in spite of* their organisation.This has implications both for how far they can pursue an empowering practice and for the methods and tactics that will best help to develop it.

Having said that, if the practice of workers is to be guided by ideas of involvement and empowerment and not just confused by them, they must first be clear what this means. There are four important dimensions to an empowering practice.

1. **The aim of practice is to empower people** – challenging oppression and discrimination rather than reflecting them and making it possible for people to take greater charge of their lives.
2. **Practice offers people control in their personal dealings with agencies** – allowing them to participate in what happens to them instead of being kept in an excluding or passive relationship. Five components of practice are usually identified:

    ● assessment
    ● planning
    ● recording
    ● action
    ● review.

    Service users should be involved in them all: defining their own needs and having a say in planning and decision-making.
3. **Practice equips people to take power** – *enabling* them to participate by helping them gain the confidence, self-esteem, assertiveness, expectations, knowledge and skills needed to have an effective say.
4. **The agency in which practice is located is open to people's involvement** – offering opportunities, structures and resources for a say in its working.

So an empowering practice ideally puts people in a position to have more say and offers the first and most concrete expression of their involvement. Counselling, rights work and information-giving can all form part of an empowering practice. For example, one of us has worked as a volunteer face-to-face counsellor with people with HIV and AIDS. Many people with AIDS may initially feel they have lost control of their lives. Counselling can help them get back that control and live positively while facing many possible changes.

In this chapter we will mainly be concerned with the first two dimensions we have identified. We discuss the others elsewhere in the book. But what would an empowering practice actually look like? People's own views and experience of empowering and disempowering practice hold important clues. Let's begin with some of the things they've told us. First a self-help group of parents with children in care:

'You do not know where you are with social workers. They often totally fail to understand what it's like for a parent to lose a child by going into care . . . It's very difficult for parents to feel they could have any say in social services. Social workers have tremendous power over people which they do not always recognise . . . You feel helpless in the face of social workers.'

Next a woman who wrote to us, who had had to retire early after long experience of mental distress:

'Unfortunately my feelings are that I NEVER had a say in anything that was happening to me . . . The only way I seem relieved is being with someone I constantly trust and who stays supportive, calm and consistent and capable. (Oh horror when very occasionally I distrust this person and start thinking – what if they're going to arrange I go to hospital?) . . . I found a clinic that spent ages teaching me to know myself, to develop a strong centre and to have strategies to watch out for going too high or low. It sounds simple, but I've been really well ever since. I no longer take any medication. . . . I work locally with other consumers and have very good feedback. In all cases, I find people want: (a) MY TIME and (b) MY ATTENTION. I think the VERY BEST help I've ever got has been either when I'm listened to and taken seriously, or when I've found something helpful by my own searching and negotiation . . . . What so much of these wretched institutions and workers do is work out "what's best for the client". I keep asking if they consult with the client and then the room goes dead quiet!'

Finally a group of homeless people at a day centre:

'Social security, they say it's in the post and when you see the post mark, it's the night before . . . Not advising you of all

the things you're entitled to. You've got to find out. They should explain or refer you to a social worker. You need continuing communication, information. There's talk of social services having problems with cut backs, understaffed. I don't think it's only that. Lack of understanding, sympathy, lack of empathy. Being treated badly demoralises you, aggravates you, erodes you. When people do take the trouble, it is appreciated. Treat people with respect.'

Principles for an empowering practice

There is no definitive list of principles for empowerment, but a number kept cropping up in the comments of both service users and practitioners. Some may just seem principles for good rather than specifically empowering practice, if such a distinction can be drawn. All may appear self-evident to some readers, but judging by the difficulties described by people using services, they are often absent. Together they offer practitioners a way of changing the balance of power both within and beyond their practice. An empowering practice begins by treating people with equality and can lead to their taking more control. Let's begin by headlining three of these principles.

● give people a choice of who works with them
● start with a clear and agreed code of practice
● present people in positive not demeaning images.

Next let's look more closely at five others.

Listen to what people say

Earlier in the book, when we were looking at information-gathering and consultation, we talked about the importance of setting up structures and organising meetings and events in a way which would help people to be listened to. We have also touched on the importance of *listening* for people seeking to increase their own say. But it is also helpful for workers to look more carefully at their own personal listening. The adviser working with people with learning difficulties we quoted earlier has had some important things to say about this:

> 'Listening is something we tend to do automatically, without thinking consciously about it, particularly when we are with people of similar interests and background who "speak our language"; it rarely occurs to us that we might need to develop our listening skills; but if we did, some of us might become better listeners!
>
> . . . really listening to someone who is a newcomer to the group, and whose opportunities to develop conversational skills, think logically and get a message across clearly may have been severely limited, requires a deliberate effort on our part and even the development of new skills.
>
> For example the person with learning difficulties may say something which seems to be way off the point. But a good listener will often be able to detect a link. It might be the last word said by another person present. The person with learning difficulties has picked this up and related it to his/her own experience in some way. Other members of the group need to discover what this link might be – building on it to draw out something meaningful to the rest of the discussion.
>
> The baseline must always be "Have we explained this carefully enough?" or 'Have we provided all the support this person needs in order to participate in the discussions?' It should never be, "Oh (s)he can't be expected to understand that idea or that document."' (Whittaker, 1990)

Keep people informed

Not being kept in the picture was a major bugbear among the users of services we spoke to. Never assume that people don't want to know what's happening. Practice should be explicit rather than covert. Explore your own reasons for not telling people something. Say what you are doing, keep people in touch with developments, explain the options, let them know what's likely to happen, be honest about any problems and share any information that's available. How else can they reach a rational judgement or decision and come to any real agreement with you?

Offer people support, not direction

The worker's aim should be to help people work out what they want and enable them to play an active part in achieving it. They, not the worker, should be the arbiter of what is needed. One example from social work has been the increased use of written and negotiated agreements between people and practitioners which are open to amendment on both sides. This approach suggests a shift in professional philosophy. It does not deny the worker's skills but may indicate a different kind – enabling rather than directive. This is what a worker in a project for people with HIV and AIDS said:

> **'It's giving them control, but not just doing what they want. You'll say to them, that's what I think is the best thing, based on my professional skill and if they say "No way I'll have that", OK, that's how it is. It's a constant negotiation.'**

Here is how one citizen advocate expressed it:

> **'You work alongside people with stigmatised identities to strengthen their position, to improve their lives, instead of taking over from them and actually denying their chances to speak for themselves.'**

Some people, like her, question whether services could ever work like this. Others, like us, feel their future lies in this direction.

See the whole person in context

Take account of people's social and other circumstances. Be sensitive to issues of race, class, gender, age, disability and sexuality. People don't exist in isolation. They aren't just a set of symptoms. It's important not to treat them as though they were. Two women spoke of their experience of psychiatric services which failed to see them in their totality.

'I think they see your distress too simply. Like – you must have lost a relative, or your money or something. But there are heaps of other stresses – marriage, being a woman in changing times, unemployment, family position.'

'The doctors just treated my symptoms and didn't attempt to see my difficulties as part of a distressed family and they prescribed drugs like Smarties to a young girl unaware of addictive side effects and withdrawal syndrome.'

Enable reciprocity and exchange

People have strengths as well as vulnerabilities. They should be able to give as well as receive. A worker with young people said:

'What assumptions are made about people coming to social services – that they have deficits. How true is this? We need to challenge it.

Instead of confirming dependence, practice should enable people's partnership. There should be a two-way traffic of understanding and experience. Service users are often *distanced* from service providers. There is much talk among professionals of 'setting boundaries'. Social workers are warned against being 'sucked in' by 'clients' who 'want to blur the distinction' and see them as friend and confidant. But as two women said, writing about social work and refugees:

'Others will be baffled by someone who feels it is unprofessional to reveal details about their personal life. Many women are used to getting and giving support to other women. A Latin-American woman with this expectation might feel that if she confides her marital difficulties to a female social worker, the worker will reciprocate by sharing her own similar experiences . . . How would you respond to a Chilean client who wants to know if your husband is unfaithful too?' (Finlay and Reynolds, 1987)

Rights and empowerment

The starting point of efforts to improve people's treatment has usually been defining their rights. Some welfare agencies now enshrine these in users' charters, confirming people's right to personal dignity, independence, choice, their own cultural, religious, sexual and emotional needs and so on. Three categories of rights have been identified: human and legal rights and rights to services (NCVO, 1984). At its narrowest, a rights approach may be a matter of formal processes, complex documentation and quasi-legalistic adversarial situations few of us are equipped to handle. In the past an emphasis on individual rights has sometimes been polarised against the achievement of collective ones. A more pressing problem is how to turn paper rights into *real* ones. The two ways of doing this are for people to be able to secure their own rights and for them to have support to obtain them, from either inside or outside the agency. These are the self-advocacy and professional advocacy models we have discussed.

In our view, self-advocacy is likely to be the most effective way of both achieving and defining our rights. There are also limits to the extent to which workers can act as advocates for users of their own agency. But an empowering practice can build a bridge between the two approaches, by encouraging initiatives for individual and group self-advocacy and supporting people to gain the confidence and skills they need. A worker who was trying to facilitate self-advocacy in her area said:

> 'It might not be right for me to be trying to involve people. They might feel suspicious of me, linked with the social services department. What would be better is if we could get money for a community development worker who was independent to find out what people are doing and work alongside groups.'

A welfare rights officer described a model of professional advocacy which involved people, instead of taking over from them; addressing the tension between advocating for someone and enabling them to speak for themselves.

'Sometimes at tribunals, I end up saying very little because the appellant is articulate, has grasped the point of legal argument and presents the case very well – other times, the appellants lack confidence; are unable to articulate themselves; are unable to speak English; do not begin to grasp that it is necessary (unfortunately) to present a legal argument and not simply an emotive one; and/or expressly wish someone to speak for them . . . I don't think welfare rights is about doing things for people . . . It is about disseminating information in a more accessible way . . . providing support and guidance to people without becoming colonialist about it. Equipping people, either individually or in groups to deal with agencies . . . It should be about providing a back-up service to those that need it.'

Workers also talked of the narrow line between enabling people to speak for themselves and leaving them to knock at the door of an intractable agency which took much more notice of *them*. Their role here may be to challenge this, instead of leaving service users at its mercy.

Let's now focus on four rights issues that have particular importance in personal services.

● complaints procedures
● data protection
● access to records
● participation in the decision-making process.

Running through them is a theme common to all rights. People need to be **aware** of their rights and have **skills** and **support** to make the most of them.

Complaints procedures

A more participatory practice can prevent things going wrong, but if they do, it's important that people can obtain redress. One expression of the growing interest in consumerism in British welfare services has been renewed activity in relation to complaints procedures. They have their limitations. They can only help when things have already gone wrong. Agencies seem to see them as much as a way of protecting themselves as their users. People need the chance to comment, not just to complain. Such mechanisms may make little difference if the balance of power remains unchanged. However they have their part to play.

If they are to be helpful, they should be seen as part of a policy of empowerment, not an alternative to it – what one commentator called 'a necessary but last step in a process of accountability and involvement'.

There are many barriers which stop people from complaining. It doesn't occur to them. They are reluctant to. It seems a waste of time. We were told of an agency where people with a complaint were advised to get in touch with the chair of the committee who then handed it back to the manager originally concerned. One disabled man talked about people's fears of reprisals and the withdrawal of services they depended on. The group of parents with children in care said:

'Complaints procedures are limited in their effectiveness as long as they are an internal process. Sometimes in a child care case, the whole department has been involved, right up to the Director.'

Experts and rights and users' organisations identify several crucial components for effective complaints procedures. They should:

● resolve minor problems informally
● be well publicised, so that people know about them
● be clearly set out, so they can be understood
● be accessible
● be independent and include the right of external appeal, to ensure fair and proper treatment
● offer independent advocacy, to help people frame and pursue their complaints
● be rapid, with fixed time limits
● be regularly monitored as a basis for improving practice and services
● have their recommendations accepted by agencies.

Data protection

Data protection and access to records legislation in Britain offer some baselines for more open practice. But issues of access and confidentiality go much further. A former worker with a project for young people said:

> 'People must feel in control of information they give. No information would be disclosed to another agency without the permission of the young person. Although as a voluntary project we needed to keep the respect of agencies like the police, probation and social services, we kept to this.'

A local authority officer for people with HIV/AIDS told us:

> 'Confidentiality is a big issue. It's been brought into focus by the disastrous consequences there have been from lack of it – for example, actual physical harassment – the whole thing about files being left lying around the office . . . It's been agreed here that it will not be recorded on a child's file if he/ she is HIV-positive as too many people get access to children's files.'

Access to records

A woman involved in developing access to records policy in one social services department emphasised the importance of a *'pro-active'* access policy.

> 'Few people ask to see their files. It should be "would you like to see your files?", not you having to ask . . . . If it's a matter of "you can write in", rather than "do you want to see your files?", it's a big performance. Then people are unlikely to want to see them. It's not conducive to seeing them. It's not the same as the social worker saying "I'd really like to share my work with you" . . . I see access as a way of preventing things going wrong. I expect more complaints with people knowing what's being written about them . . . How is the social worker going to deal with the difficulties? It's more

confronting, more testing of their professionalism. We're not used to sharing our views. It's very much about social workers having to be upfront, open, assertive confident . . . If you are practising próperly you're recording things. You're evidencing things. You are saying why you are coming to conclusions. You are explaining why you are recording something.'

The organiser of a voluntary welfare project working with families wrote:

'We encourage people to write to us knowing that their communications will also be available to the families concerned. Because of course, our client is sometimes principally a young child we have to reluctantly accept that some information remains confidential . . . My personal expect-ation is that the confidential section of any file will increas-ingly be smaller. It is worth mentioning that a great number of files do not have any confidential material in them . . . Sometimes there is also an issue of whose file [it is]. Families have a habit of splitting up and of course we would not reveal the address, for example, of a woman who was fleeing domestic violence to a man she was once living with.'

Open records again raise the issue of *language*. They won't mean much if language is still excluding, discriminatory, judgemental and jargon-filled. This is what one welfare service user said:

'They use words you don't know. Interviewers are surprised if you use the same words. They should try and explain in a simpler fashion. It's to confuse you and to try and make you walk away. It emphasises their position of power.'

We need to reflect on the language we use. Where does it come from? How do we talk about people? Some guidelines may be helpful. For example:

● Include as part of agency policy on access to records the use of accessible language.

● Listen to people's own preferences for language, terms and definitions to describe themselves.
● Stop using initials and acronyms especially in the presence of service users.
● Include language on the training agenda instead of taking it for granted.
● Look again at how you think and talk about service users. How much do you see them as a separate entity and attach generalised characteristics to them?

In its narrowest sense, access to records policy may only mean a duty to disclose some of the information kept about people. But it can mean much more. Some of its advocates emphasise much broader links between access, recording and a more equal and participatory practice which demystifies and changes the relationship between people and professionals. In one intermediate treatment project, for example, young people were involved in writing their own monthly progress reports with staff. One young person wrote his on his own. The development worker we have already heard from described her authority's approach to shared recording.

'From experience, if you involve people in recording in a positive way, they will welcome it. It changes the whole nature of what they think we social workers are. They can get your role right . . . It's worked very well with people with learning difficulties, giving people power to feel they can be responsible for their lives. If a person has senile dementia maybe they can't share it, but the carer could, using a record as *terra firma* to help orientate people . . . I prefer if the client writes in their bits, but that's not happening yet. I suggest telling the client, "I'm filling in one of these. I'll take it away, have my bit typed in and bring it back so you can see it. This is your opportunity to write what you feel your problem is. It may not be the same as what I feel it is." You have to help them feel comfortable about that. There's a need for an advocate, an independent helper to help people to write their bit. Invite them to have a friend present, someone they trust.

It should be seen as a fundamental issue of social work practice. By sharing records you're equalising the balance of power, changing the state of knowledge. It changes your practice when you get faced by the client. It's to do with practice, not just recording. It's a participatory thing. It's all about our definitions of what social work is – what is good social work.'

Participation in the decision-making process

When the people they work with participate in decision-making, practitioners must be much more rigorous about their opinions and judgements and more open about the reasons for their actions. A major focus of concern in social work has been the right of families and children to participate in child protection case conferences and reviews. Pressure has also mounted for young people's statutory right of involvement in childcare reviews to be more than a paper exercise. Child protection is the most contentious area of social work practice and raises wider issues of participation with particular intensity. This is what members of the self-help group of parents with children in care said:

'We'd like to see more parents involved in case conferences, so we can find out the real reasons for what social services do. Otherwise it's all cut and dried before you get in there . . . Our experience is not so much about challenging decisions but involving parents and allowing them to bring a friend along from the group. Once a parent comes to a case conference, almost invariably a *better* decision is made, even if it's not always the one a parent wants.'

Studies suggest most parents and staff feel that better plans and decisions are made when parents are present. A social services area officer and team leader who both chaired child protection case conferences said:

'The benefits are that you can be open. People will know where they stand. You know what people are saying about your child and your care of it and what you need to change,

what other people are doing to help you change and what will happen if you don't . . .You get the chance to see all the people involved, hear what they're saying . . . We're beginning to get together all the people chairing these conferences to have joint training – how we do it, involving parents, keeping the needs of the child in focus . . . The role of the chair is to enable all participants to participate, parents, professionals, foster parents . . . Where parents seem to be genuinely involved in the debate is where they have had real discussion with the worker before. They're not unaware of the plans, what people think. They're prepared for it. Where there's been a difficulty in openness anyway, it can feel like the only opportunity for parents to have a go at people.'

Clearly, to be effective, people's involvement in such decision-making needs to be part of a more empowering practice, not an island apart from it. Welfare rights workers, service users and researchers also identify a range of requirements if people's involvement in meetings is to be more than tokenistic. They should:

be notified in advance of any meeting concerning them
be kept fully informed of what's happening
be given all relevant information in advance
be offered any practical help they need to participate, including childcare and transport
be welcomed and introduced to other participants have access to a free and independent advocacy service
be properly briefed in advance about the meeting's process, agenda and other participants so they can make an effective contribution
receive a record of the meeting.

Challenges to empowerment

Social work and social services highlight three other important issues which have ramifications for an open and empowering practice.

● stigma and dependency
● violence
● people's involvement when their rights are restricted.

Let's look at each of them briefly.

Stigma and dependency

Sucking people into stigmatising services is the opposite of empowerment. They should be able to get help and resources without being 'clientised' or defined as dependent. As the social services department area officer said:

'I feel the issue about stigma and dependency starts from the way social services structure themselves and present themselves to the public. I feel very aware of this issue at a time when we are considering reorganising on specialist lines. This will mean that the Department is structured according to individual and family disabilities so there will be managers for mental illness (health and disability), elderly people, teams for child protection, etc.

My own belief . . . is that we should be trying to offer an all-embracing service where clients/members of the public requesting social services are empowered to define those services they wish to receive. They should not have to be stigmatised into a pigeon-hole before they qualify for a service. After the service is structured according to "disability" and services are budgeted according to "disability", then you are likely to be building up a fairly stigmatised and dependent system.'

Registration on the child protection register, for instance, shouldn't be parents' only avenue to support services.

'If we are involving parents in a way that doesn't just write them off, it takes resources at an early stage, family centres etc, going beyond "Can this parent manage on income support with a difficult child?" The whole procedure thing has become so important. The conference has become all important. Where is the prevention aspect in all this? Better practice takes more resources. The move is to a crisis service away from a preventive service.'

Violence

Some social workers have been murdered by service users. Many more suffer verbal and physical abuse and violence. It's a problem that workers, particularly women workers, also face in other services like schools, social security and housing offices. When services deteriorate, staff become the meat in the sandwich between them and their increasingly frustrated users. Different approaches have been adopted to deal with violence. Workers may be taught physical skills or techniques for avoiding and calming anger and outbursts. Environments may be more closely controlled to protect workers, although fortifying them with metal grilles, reinforced glass and fixed furniture may actually have the opposite effect. This is what the social services area officer said:

'It is in both the way workers talk to users of the service, and the way the environment values users that violence is likely to be reduced. If the environment is positive and clearly expects positive behaviour; if waiting times are reduced and users are treated with respect, then the violence will be reduced. Controlling environments are definitely counter-productive. This does not mean that you cannot have wise precautions like panic buttons.

There is also the important issue that workers should not allow themselves to become victims of the system, or victims of poor resources. If there is a dangerous situation to go to, they should be properly supported. They should be able to go out in pairs, there should be hand-held telephone sets available, there should be a duty senior on contact, etc. If violence is threatened to staff, it should be responded to properly. Clients have no entitlement to be violent any more than workers. Departments need to have proper policies on violence which, if necessary, may mean sanctions being

taken. Within a proper policy framework workers will feel more secure.'

A more open and empowering practice also has a part to play. It's no panacea. But it can help to prevent and defuse aggression by *challenging* instead of adding to people's sense of powerlessness and low self-worth.

People's involvement when their rights are restricted

People who are sceptical about participation and empowerment regularly return to one fundamental issue. It's generally put something like this:

> **'It's all very well to talk about involving people and *their* right to a say. What about people who infringe *other* people's rights or are a danger to themselves or others? How does it fit with that?'**

It's a difficult question which shouldn't be ducked. It's especially important for social and other services which have a duty both to protect and restrict people's rights. First, let's draw a distinction. Service workers shouldn't confuse their care and control roles. As one child protection study reported, parents knew social workers were visiting to check on their children's care. What they found frustrating was them pretending to be in their preferred role of helpers (Corby, 1987). Workers should be honest and open with themselves and those they work with about their regulatory role.

Terms like 'consumer' and 'customer' may seem even less appropriate for their users once we acknowledge this. But interventions that restrict people's rights don't have to and shouldn't exclude their involvement. It's needed *more than ever* in such circumstances. The question is not so much how you reconcile people's involvement with restrictions on their rights as how justice can be done if people are denied any say or involvement in such decisions. In childcare legislation, the pendulum has swung between children's and parental rights as successive childcare tragedies and scandals have pulled it one way and another. But the abrogation of parental rights and involvement has rarely meant that children's were safe-guarded any better. Where people's rights are in question, their involvement and empowerment are essential to ensure that:

● they and their representatives can put their case
● they are involved in the making of the decision
● they are fully aware of what decision is made and why
● they can appeal against decisions
● they are involved in the review of decision.

Support for an empowering practice

Practitioners need support to work in a more open and empowering way. One woman with mental distress high-lighted how different practice could look from opposite sides of the counter:

'I was working as a nurse in hospitals before it happened. Seeing from both sides was an experience in itself . . . On my patient side, I saw clusters of doctors, nurses, physios at bay doors, talking very quietly; straining to hear if you make out any little word. On my nurse side, sharing information, discussing treatments, no feeling of locking patient out. We're in control. Patient wouldn't know what we are talking about anyway. As a patient, bombarding to get information, and need to know, to understand, something concrete. As the nurse being pestered by patient. You've got thirty other patients to deal with, time for really ill patients. Patient wants painkillers. As nurse, why didn't they say in last drug round, or wait till next, now got to get keys, as if you haven't enough to do. Patient feels rejected and an inconvenience. Nurse: you are a pain. Patient keeps a look out for a favourite nurse to ask. Nurse, been noticed, told to spend less time with patient.'

Public service workers may have far-reaching powers over the rest of us, but they often feel powerless in their own organisation. If they are to help empower others, they must first be empowered themselves. That means respecting their rights and placing a greater emphasis on more participatory models of management. As we said earlier, it's not enough to press for service users' involvement in isolation. We heard a politician at a conference using self-advocacy as a stick to beat professionals. Complaints procedures are unlikely to work if they aren't agreed with workers. Workers too must have more say if people's participation is to be effective and not divisive.

Practitioners also need training, resources and information. How, for example, can they help people use their agency, if they don't **know** how to negotiate it themselves? They want independent advisers to help change their way of working, just like service users. They often feel they do good work *despite* their organisation. Their commitment to empower service users may run counter to the organisation's culture.

What we have learned from talking with workers trying to pursue an empowering practice in both sympathetic and unsympathetic organisations is the importance of knowing your organisation and making links with kindred spirits within and beyond it. Alliances are one way in which practitioners can gain support to deal with the pressures and problems they face. Developing their own networks will reduce their isolation and encourage the exchange of experience and ideas. Closer partnership between professionals and non-professionals makes possible mutual training and brings together professional skills and citizen knowledge; professional resources and citizen networks. By becoming allies of user and rights organisations, practitioners can get support as well as giving it.

In the next chapter we look at *policy* for citizen involvement and empowerment. One of the issues we shall explore is the kind of relationship there needs to be between agencies and workers if it's to work.

9

Towards a Policy for Citizen Involvement

We began this book by talking about people's right to a greater say in their lives, services and neighbourhoods. Now we end by looking at policies which can help make this possible. We have already examined many of their components. We still have to see how these might actually fit together and be best implemented. While we start with the agencies people use, we soon find ourselves drawn to much broader issues. Citizen involvement and empowerment can't be considered in isolation. That's one reason why the development of policy poses some difficult questions. Let's begin with a few of these.

How do you make change to give people greater control? Is it the same as making any other change, as some commentators suggest? How do you translate involvement and empowerment into an agency strategy? Some people argue you can't. The usual route taken has been changed structures and new bricks and mortar. This may be easier and more visible than other approaches, but that doesn't mean it works. We studied a major reorganisation of social services which was meant to give people more say in them. But they weren't involved in the process of change and subsequently felt as powerless as before (Beresford and Croft, 1986). One consultant on consumer involvement told us:

'There's a feeling that the way to do it is to reorganise people. You can do it till the cows come home and nothing will

177

change. You've got to change the *culture*. You've got to focus on the process of arriving at policies.'

Let's say there's a commitment to offer people more say and involvement. How do we get beyond pilot projects and individual enthusiasms to embed people's participation in the *fabric* of an agency or organisation? How do we prevent it dying when a worker moves on or special funding ends? A researcher monitoring such a situation said:

'One view is that you build it into the existing bureaucratic procedures. Another, that if you do that, it'll bureaucratise the whole process.'

Finally, how can developments in one field be extended to others? HIV and AIDS has highlighted this for social services. A social services department AIDS officer said:

'What we've seen happen is that lots of other people working in social services say, "But why are we only doing this for people with AIDS?" This is a new problem affecting a new group of people so we've had to think about what we can offer. AIDS has been the peg on which we've had to address lots and lots of issues . . . For example, the way people with AIDS who have dementia are treated and the interest shown in dealing with this will have a helpful knock-on effect for elderly people. We have a chance to get it right now. And if we get it right for this group of people, maybe we can get it right for others . . . There is a positive side. It is easy to say that as someone who doesn't have AIDS and who hasn't suffered obviously, but I think good things can come out of the AIDS issue in terms of services. It has shown how positive it has been involving users and it has brought the whole issue of homosexuality and sex back on to the agenda as well.'

Borrowing from business

There are no simple answers. Model policies to increase people's say and involvement have yet to be discovered, assuming they exist. Meanwhile, agencies trying to get closer

to the public have taken conventional consumerism as their
first port of call. They have appropriated slogans like
'customer care', 'aiming for excellence' and 'quality service'
from the business world to express their increased concern for
their constituents. They have borrowed basic business checklists like:

first identify who your actual and potential customers are
check why they aren't using your service
what is your image?
what is your product?
how might they need to change?

Health and welfare services shopping for more consumer-
orientated policies have also comprehensively raided modern
business managerialism. Some of the policies and principles
they have adopted are explicitly concerned with increasing
consumer-involvement. Others are offered as helpful ways of
fostering and encouraging it. They include:

clarifying the agency mission
quality assurance – through standard setting, inspection,
regulation, audit and evaluation
performance related pay
● devolved budgets
customer feedback – including information-gathering and
consultation
including representatives of the target market in management structures
flatter management structures – giving local managers
greater control within centrally set parameters and improving vertical and horizontal communication
● recruitment, promotion and training consistent with
agency culture.

But policies like these also bring us back to some of the
conflicts and confusions between consumerism and empowerment. For instance, the benefits of devolved budgets for
community and rights groups, might be a greater say in
expenditure and more accessible grant-giving processes. But

what they more often mean is the creation of 'cost centres' and increased local managerial budgetary discretion and responsibility within centrally determined objectives. The two are very different. One starts from the agency's interests; the other from those of its users. Performance-related pay raises similar issues. Its advocates present it as an effective carrot-and-stick approach to improved customer service. Its critics condemn it for replacing collective negotiation with individual incentives. So far audit been mainly been concerned with the *agency's* three *E*s – economy, efficiency and effectiveness, rather than *people's* three *P*s – participation, partnership and power-sharing.

While the origins of such approaches may be closer managerial control, they don't have to stop there. They are open to wide interpretation. For example, the setting of performance review targets can be a two-way process, instead of them just cascading down from above. People's performance may be judged on a team basis, encouraging teamwork instead of individual competition. Conditions to ensure people's involvement can be included in contracts. In one area, 'purchaser' and 'provider' agencies have jointly funded an independent users' group which is involved in planning and designing contracts for mental health services (Barker, 1991).

Consumerism can come closer to empowerment than we may realise. Many of the managerialist methods we have outlined can be put to empowering uses. What is essential is to be clear about your objectives, understand the ambiguities of consumerist approaches and then adapt them accordingly. We saw this in some of the participatory initiatives we encountered. They show how approaches which have their roots in managerialism can nonetheless support people's empowerment.

Coherent policy for people's say and involvement

We haven't come across many agencies which have developed comprehensive policies to increase people's say and involvement. Initiatives are more often confined to one service, one aspect of involvement, one group of service users, one locality, or one-off schemes. Those we have encountered show just how many components may be required and the variety of approaches possible. They include agency-led, user-led and collaborative ventures. This is where issues of organisational change and personal empowerment meet. Participatory initiatives must address both. We can see agencies trying to work through and reconcile the sometimes conflicting values and demands of the two.

It will be helpful to look in greater detail at some of these more comprehensive policies. But first a word of warning. All are subject to change. None claims to offer the answer. Their initiators are often at pains to point this out:

> **'One of the important things I have to emphasise is that participation isn't effective here yet. It's a goal we have to work towards.'**

> **'I don't think we've got it all right by any means. I think we are just further along that road.'**

This raises another issue. We have found that the most self-critical initiatives are often the most impressive and far-reaching. Unfortunately, the ambiguities of participation mean that it still tends to be those making the biggest claims which are the most visible and most often imitated. So buyer beware! But all face the same difficulties in ensuring people's involvement and escaping the almost limitless ability of organisations to subvert it.

We can also begin to understand why there seem to be relatively few comprehensive schemes when we look at just how many conditions may be needed for them to develop. Take this small community project in which local people involved expressed a real sense of ownership and control. These are some of the factors they told us it took to get it off the ground:

● the project was in a designated area eligible for special funding
● community work had strong credibility in the authority
● the community work team leader had a long track record, which included previous work in the area.

the project had the support and encouragement of other team members, senior managers, politicians of both political parties and a local district advisory committee.

it was protected by a key member of the social services committee who chaired the finance subcommittee, had local contacts and could enlist sympathetic local professionals on to a project steering group

the existence of a good relationship between social services and housing helped provide premises

contact had already been made with some local residents

a community worker was employed to involve and support local people.

Now let's turn to our examples.

A policy for people with learning difficulties

The first of these is a social service department initiative to increase the say and involvement of people with learning difficulties in their lives and services. It's part of a regional strategy to develop services with their users' involvement. The principal officer concerned stressed four requirements to achieve this: changing the agency's culture, developing structures, policies and opportunities for participation, raising people's expectations that they will be consulted; and recognising that change takes time. These are some of the steps that have been taken:

Creating a joint secretariat responsible for all service developments for people with learning difficulties, made up of senior managers from health, social services and education departments, together with representatives of voluntary organisations, service users and their families.

Establishing a local policy framework where funding for services is conditional on the involvement of service users.

Setting up local planning and coordination groups to plan and develop services, made up of local managers and representatives of parents and service users, with a small budget to enable participation.

Setting up service user committees for all services.

Setting up self-advocacy groups to support people involved in local planning groups.

Providing training on participation for staff, service users and their parents.

Providing information to direct and indirect service users.

Requiring written and verbal reports on progress with participation, giving feedback and making written reports available.

In one area, establishing a consumer representatives' group for all service users on the local planning and coordinating group to support them to report back to other people.

A principal officer committed to participation, who spends a day in each of the services for which he is responsible once every six months, talking with service users and workers.

Involving service users in decisions about their individual needs and how they are met.

Running workshops for people with learning difficulties to evaluate the quality of the service they receive.

Setting up a county-wide evaluation group involving direct and indirect service users.

Making commitment to participation a key criterion for promotion.

Developing services with disabled people

Disabled people are a group who have had a particularly coherent approach to gaining more control over their lives and services. The next example offers a powerful illustration of this.

Disabled people set up a county-wide coalition of disabled people which they controlled.

Their demands rested on a clear philosophy based on a social model of disability. This conceives the problem of disability as lying in the relationship between disabled and non-disabled people. Seven needs were identified which collectively formed the framework for the development of services to enable the participation of disabled people in mainstream life and activities: information, counselling, housing, transport, access, technical aids and personal assistance.

In the International Year of Disabled People (1981), the coalition proposed setting up a centre for integrated living to provide services for people wishing to live integrated lives in the community.

Strong formal and informal links were developed with supportive politicians and officers

The local authority signed a statement of intent and adopted a strategic plan to promote the participation of disabled people. The social services department established a disability project to work out changed relationships between service providers and users and develop services to support their social integration.

The local authority established a disabled persons unit within the equal opportunities and race relations department.

The centre for integrated living was an autonomous organisation which received its main funding from the county council and the European Community Social Fund.

It fitted into a wider strategy for county council services for disabled people which rested on the principle of joint participation between disabled people and statutory agencies and shared control of service design and delivery.

The joint planning group which included representatives of the health authority, social services, coalition and centre for integrated living, rejected a proposed younger disabled persons unit in favour of community services and flexible budgets.

The governing body of the centre for integrated living included representatives of the county council, coalition and local voluntary organisations. At least half its members were disabled people.

Access to records policy

Next we hear from the development worker involved in an agency-wide access to records policy:

'The principal officer was a key person in pushing it. You need someone to keep it alive all the time, otherwise it'll die. He got the University in as consultants. The director was supportive. One of the area organisers worked very hard on the groundwork to make sure our policy got as far as it did. He set up a working group. It did a lot of work. It identified the need to be pro-active. We started with two areas. We went to a national conference on access to records to find out what was going on elsewhere. We established guidelines. A group was set up to design them, mostly team leaders. I was one of them, I was then a social worker.

I was seconded for a year full-time to be involved in training. We trained key staff in two day sessions – all people responsible for staff, officers-in-charge, seniors. We had a training pack to familiarise teams and workers before it became policy. I went round teams by invitation. I went to them rather than waiting for them to respond. It's not enough to expect some key workers to spread the word. I'm not saying there was resistance, but there was anxiety. You should do it from the start in basic training. It's about changing attitudes. You also need specific courses. I know of one professional course which includes client access. Recording is now being built into the local course. Practice teacher training should also include it.

We had meetings with other agencies involved; housing, police, education, health. It really helped to offload fears and break down barriers. As well as the training pack and programme, we produced a leaflet for users. We had a monitoring group meeting monthly. It was an opportunity to shape guidelines in the light of experience and to keep area representatives in touch. It's a policy that's difficult to monitor. It's more subtle. Social workers were interested, but it wasn't imperative to grapple with it. Seniors are the key. I don't think more could be done in training. It's the operational follow-up. To what extent could we make it a requirement, monitor it and deal with shortcomings? If you impose it, then people just do a different defensive kind of recording. How could you reinforce people for doing it properly? My social workers would be rewarded for sharing

records when they come to evaluation for upgrading. I feel
that ultimately the pressure will come from service users.'

Older people's participation in residential services

This initiative to increase older people's participation in local
authority residential homes is more modest than the others we
describe. This makes it typical of many more. It also shows
how important small scale schemes can be in turning policy
into practice. One of the homes' managers was seconded to
the project for one day a fortnight for a few months. This is
what he said:

'The Department established a charter of residents' rights,
including the right to be fully informed about services, to be
consulted about daily living arrangements and to participate
in discussions about any proposed changes in them. In this
home, we have a residents' meeting every three weeks, chaired
by an independent person from a voluntary organisation.
They're not just about the menu, or the bed not being
made, but other crucial issues. Staff are only present when
requested. Residents are involved in appointments and they
control the residents' fund. In addition to the key worker
system, which can break down with sickness, someone acts as
information person, going round once a week, letting people
know what's going on on an individual and group basis.

I was asked to do an audit of consumer involvement in
homes in the division. I made a small-scale survey of staff and
residents. I looked at information, staff commitment and
customer involvement; what staff felt about participation,
how useful residents' meetings were, what kind of decisions
were made. Asking people, "Could you say anything if your
room wasn't cleaned or you saw someone assaulted?"

There's a lot of variation. We've got a departmental
mandate for participation. We need to build in practical
mechanisms. Staff are mostly keen on residents participating
more. Where the atmosphere of a home is for participation,
residents are more *au fait* with it.

We're setting up a working party in each home. The report we've produced makes some specific recommendations about how we can improve consultation. How do I feel? Depends if I'm sitting in a room with 20 people criticising you. I felt the atmosphere made that possible for them, that no one's going to jump down their throat, but after I left, I felt, thank God I've got a good supportive line manager. You need that. They understand and know things take time.'

Policy for people with HIV and AIDS

Finally, these are some of the elements involved in a social services department initiative to develop policy for people with HIV and AIDS in partnership with them.

1. **Additional funding** allocated from central government.
2. **Social services HIV policy and practice group** – a departmental group, meeting monthly, concerned with policy and practice development around AIDS. It is chaired by the deputy director and includes front-line staff and members of organisations of people with AIDS.
3. **Joint planning team** – bringing together representatives of social services, housing, the health authority, organisations of people with AIDS and other agencies. Their task is to develop a strategy on AIDS for social services, health authority and voluntary organisations, offering a model for good practice, service development and resources. It has a number of subgroups and working parties all of which have representatives from organisations of people with AIDS.
4. **Cross-party political support** and support from senior management and staff.
5. **Staff support groups** – for staff working with people with HIV and AIDS.
6. **Quality control group** – working with users of services with HIV and AIDS to develop quality targets in one social services area – 'a minimum standard of what should be provided'. It consists of managers, social

workers, relevant voluntary organisations and people with AIDS. It is also producing a booklet on making complaints.

7. **Training** – including a three-day skills course for home helps involving people from organisations of people with AIDS.

8. **A survey of people with AIDS receiving social services** – by the social services department research department to identify and explore their wants and views.

9. **Monitoring** of direct and indirect social services received by people with HIV and AIDS.

10. **The ethics group** – developed as part of the social services department monitoring system to act as a watchdog on data collection, over issues of confidentiality, etc. It is convened by the department and has five members, including one service user and two representatives of local voluntary organisations.

Some components for comprehensive policy

As these examples underline, there are two aspects to increasing people's say and involvement in organisations: **making** and **maintaining** change. The two often demand different skills and methods. The principal officer working with people with learning difficulties articulated an approach which many effective initiatives seem to adopt intuitively or explicitly:

> **'You need a concept of change and a strategy for managing that change. A lot of people don't have a concept of change and a strategy of how to do it. One of my main interests is managing organisational change. I identify wider political factors, then I look at what to do and when, who to get in place and how to do it.'**

Advocates of social role valorisation or normalisation employ a three-stage model which is also helpful here.

1. Develop a clear personal and agency value base.
2. Look at how existing services relate to it.

3.   Work out what changes to make, as individuals, teams and organisations, to bring services closer to values.

The comprehensive initiatives to involve and empower people which we encountered point to a series of components to set against the list borrowed from modern managerialism. These include:

clear agency/project goals and values
key people, groups or bodies inside the agency dedicated to the initiative and carrying it forward
gaining widespread support for involvement within the organisation
an emphasis on citizen involvement in recruitment, training and promotion
funding conditional upon people's involvement
earmarked budgets to increase people's say and involvement
agency users' involvement in the formulation and planning of participatory initiatives
participatory management systems
development projects which feed into mainstream agency policy and practice, diffusing as well as demonstrating ideas
● a source of independent skills for training and development
continuous monitoring and evaluation.

Issues for organisations and services

They also raise some wider issues for organisations and services. Let's look at these next.

Agreeing not imposing participation

It's important that workers are involved in participatory projects and that these aren't imposed on them. Empower-

ment is one change that can't be forced on people. A local
authority training officer said:

> 'There's the director telling staff, "You've got to do user-
> involvement" and managers saying the same. That's a
> mirroring of hierarchy, not empowerment. If you feel em-
> powered yourself, it's safe to empower others, if not, it's very
> threatening.'

Involving workers offers the agency the benefit of their skills
and support and gives them a voice in changing it. Excluding
them reduces participation to just another policy imposed
from above. The result is likely to be resentment and sabotage
from below. Workers are set against service users, who
become just another boss. This is what the principal officer
working with people with learning difficulties said:

> 'You can't expect people to change overnight. They will have
> been expected, maybe required, to work in one way for years.
> If you now want a different way of working, it mustn't be just
> another prescription. It's no use rushing in and giving staff a
> bollocking if they're doing something inappropriately. Instead
> of antagonising and alienating them, it needs to be a process
> of discussion, gradually influencing people's behaviour. There
> must be sensitivity to workers who find it difficult to change
> the habits of a working lifetime, or who signed up for
> something different to what is now expected.'

Tensions between top-down and bottom-up approaches

An important distinction to draw is between 'top-down' and
'bottom-up' initiatives. Each has its strengths and weaknesses.
    One top-down initiative we saw was a large-scale local
authority project to develop a strategy for community care
informed by service users' views and experience. Its main aims
were to 'promote interdepartmental work and establish
mechanisms for long term change'. Powerful political and
organisational connections were established to do this. It
came under the direct overall control of the chief executive,

was linked to a key political subcommittee and had a small steering group of chief officers and senior health authority managers. In contrast, is a morning play centre we have used. A small group of mothers who had a job or wanted one set it up with some help from teachers. It's now run by 'the friends of the school', with a council grant for one worker and fundraising for the other. Parents pay a small charge to use it.

Top-down initiatives are more likely to command official support, resources and respect. They can bring about far-reaching changes in policy and practice. But their interests and goals aren't necessarily the same as those of the people they aim to involve. It's difficult for them to get close to the ground and project links tend to be at managerial level, whereas the impact of the agency is experienced through the practice of much lower-level workers. The question which always hangs over such initiatives is, 'What does it all boil down to in practice?' Bottom-up schemes may be much closer to people's wants and preferences, but they can expect less support and understanding from the powers-that-be and a constant struggle for resources and recognition.

Neither approach is adequate on its own. What's needed is some amalgam of the two. One manager, emphasising the importance of this issue, wrote to us:

'**The tensions, in terms of control and influence, between public authorities and communities can get terribly out of balance if adequate safeguards are absent. We have found it terribly important to have strategies and tactics for maintaining this balance and feel that any tensions should be seen as a healthy motivating factor. At the end of the day, it all boils down to power, and professionals of most sorts consciously or unconsciously want it for what I consider to be all the wrong reasons.**

It is quite difficult and very hard work to get people at both the top and bottom to hold a different vision. If you are at the top and have power, it's relatively easy to keep it. If you are somewhere near the bottom of a service organisation, your power and status come from having people below you – i.e. service users. The reasons for change have to be sound and believed, otherwise, at least in the short term, the status quo

will prevail, even if on the surface, things look different. Our experience is that the "network" of believers has to exist at both the top and the bottom for fundamental change to occur. Alternatively, it is only at times when the balance of control and influence is upset (usually politically) that progress can be made – but watch out for those with power who want to get it back later!'

The centre for integrated living and strategy for people with learning difficulties are examples which go some way towards uniting top-down and bottom-up approaches. Involvement and initiatives should begin at the bottom, but with support from above. Agencies contribute their resources and commitment. From the grass roots come day-to-day contact and expertise. Guidelines and criteria agreed between the two, can ensure coherence and continuity.

The gulf between personal development and political change

We have already emphasised the importance of people being both **supported** and **accessed** to have a greater say. But the two spheres of activity tend to be separate. We have been struck by how often those working directly with people to enable their involvement by increasing their confidence, knowledge and skills, lack an understanding of the organisational and political issues that are also involved. Similarly, those involved in more policy-orientated work are often less sensitive to personal issues and issues of personal development. The first limits the likelihood of people's involvement being effective, the second of it being broad-based. It sometimes seems as though there are two quite distinct groups involved in efforts to empower people: one with personal, the other with political agendas. Of course this isn't always true. But it's exaggerated by the practical pressures of participation. Earlier we saw in community development how the pressure to achieve tangible results is often at odds with making it possible for people to take part.

These two approaches and sets of skills must be united if efforts to increase people's say are to be successful. People involved in direct work to enable people's empowerment should be equipped with a better grasp of structural issues, the politics of participation and issues of organisational change. Those concerned with more policy-orientated work need to be familiarised with both the importance of personal empowerment and ways of achieving it.

Gulfs between service providers and users

This brings us to two other related gulfs: first between service users and workers and second, between policy makers, managers and practice. Strong pressures perpetuate this. Professionalisation tends to distance workers from users, emphasising their differences rather than their similarities. Promotion in social services, for example, tends to be away from practice and contact with service users. Policy makers and academics may have little contact in their own lives with many of the disempowered groups they are concerned with.

The 'them and us' of welfare services is one of their most disabling shortcomings, especially when the aim is to empower people. Separation breeds misconceptions and fear. We talked to managers and researchers who were frank about their lack of confidence and anxiety about relating to disabled people and people with learning difficulties because of their isolation from them. A group of homeless people stressed the importance of shared experience if social workers were to help.

There are overlaps between service users and providers to build on. Human service managers and workers are not exempt from many of the needs and problems that bring people to their doors. They may be informal carers, have experience of mental distress or addiction. They may have been in care or sexually abused themselves. Mental health service workers with experience of mental distress have now set up their own self-help group. It's important to recognise the links between people's experience and foster contact between them.

Techniques like 'service sampling', where politicians and managers get a taste of the jobs and services they run, are not enough to bridge the gaps. Three developments will help.

● Equal opportunities employment policies which increase the overlaps between service providers and users.
● Organisational structures, policies and roles which encourage rather than inhibit regular contact with agency users.
● Occupational training which places an emphasis on collaboration and partnership with people rather than passivity and professional distance.

In this way, the process of people coming together and negotiating their different perspectives, which is crucial to empowerment, can become a natural day-to-day occurrence.

Changing outcomes as well as attitudes

It won't always be possible to change the attitudes and values of individuals and agencies. Instead it may be better to focus on *outcomes*. One trainer would not run anti-racist workshops for agencies unless they were committed to implement anti-racist policies. A local authority women's unit first worried about their failure to change the attitudes of colleagues and members. Then they started to ask, 'How many lamp posts have you built to light streets at night in response to women's needs and demands?' A social worker said:

'We stopped trying to get people to think differently. Instead we made clear what was acceptable behaviour and said that behaviour which was racist would not be tolerated. Hopefully attitudes too will change over time.'

Equipping people to set their own standards for quality control and evaluation

Consumerism tends to treat user-involvement and standard setting as separate rather than related issues. But it's important that service users as well as agencies have a hand in setting performance indicators and quality targets if these are to reflect their needs and preferences and not become bureaucratised and distorted. Otherwise they may be as paternalistic and prescriptive as any other measure of agency function and performance. But if people are to take part in quality setting, they need to be *supported* with the information, confidence and skills to do so. This provides a basis for the joint monitoring and evaluation of initiatives. Without it, schemes like that of a social services department which paid elderly people to stay in a home for a week and give their comments may only reflect existing assumptions, expectations and deference.

A flexible approach to increasing people's say

Policies to empower people should be flexible and sensitive to local needs. Two issues highlight this. First is the difference between town and country.

Involving people in rural areas.   Transport is always important if people are to participate, especially for those with limited mobility and for women to travel safely at night. But it is especially important in rural areas where population is scattered and public transport poor. A rural development worker identified a wide range of issues which participatory initiatives should take into account.

'If you start with small numbers in a community, the number who could get involved are even smaller. People providing structures for involvement will argue the numbers game. They set up a meeting. No one or few come, so they don't bother. "People can't be interested." There's a need for more one-to-one work. But that may be threatening for people and it requires more resources.

People, especially if they haven't got a car, which particularly means women, can't reach or come to things. It's difficult to get a group together. To become involved you become visible. Trust takes a long time to develop because people are visible. You may not want to become visible. It can raise stigma. Traditions are deeply held. There are accepted roles and structures. People make do rather than announce their needs. Expectations are very low. Newcomers may think differently, but then there's the problem of them excluding others.

Resistance is more visible. "We don't want it in our village." There isn't the same amount of public money as in the cities. Local authorities argue economy of scale, so services are in towns. That's another hassle factor. Services for older people, for example, are run by volunteers plus subsidy in the village hall. When services are voluntary, it's difficult to articulate your concerns if the volunteer lives next door. But interesting things do happen. Perhaps it's because of the recognition that there are real problems trying to involve people in rural areas so you have to try more innovatory approaches than in town.'

People with a common need, like sickle cell disease or being a claimant, are more spread out in rural areas. This makes it more difficult for them to get together and take collective action and increases the need for support and perhaps a paid worker. The fact that people are scattered also emphasises the importance of collaboration between different authorities.

Different service providers. Different service suppliers pose different problems for people's involvement. They have different chains of accountability: public services to elected political representatives; commercial organisations, to boards and shareholders; and not-for-profit agencies to management committees and trustees. Each is subject to different tensions. In commercial services, it's between meeting need and making a profit; in public provision, between meeting the needs of service providers and service users and in not-for-profit organ-isations, between what's needed and what will get funded. Of course it's more complicated than this. In Britain, the pressure has been on public agencies to become more like commercial ones. Voluntary organisations may see themselves as representing disadvantaged groups, but as we said in Chapter 1, disabled people have drawn a distinction between organisations *of* and organisations *for* disabled people, depending on whether or not disabled people control them themselves. Participatory policies must first recognise and then tackle these different tensions and chains of accountability if they are to increase people's say and involvement.

A positive climate for experiment and risk

Trying to increase people's say and involvement is difficult. There are bound to be problems and shortcomings. Mistakes will be made. But there are strong pressures to report success instead of learning from failure. One worker said:

> **'The problem is a culture where criticism is seen as a threat. We need to see it as a positive, not something to bat off, get rid of. One of the reasons for fear of the whole idea of user-involvement is of criticism. It's a mistake.'**

We don't want to dampen people's enthusiasm. The message of this book is that we can empower ourselves and others. But we won't do it by glossing over the very real difficulties we can expect to encounter. There's a temptation to report results early, as if hopes will ultimately be reflected in achievements. We have just read that one flawed scheme we visited is planning to produce how-to-do-it packs for other organisations before it has even been properly evaluated itself! Empowerment is a delicate plant which shouldn't be displayed before it has put down strong roots. It's important for funders and policy makers to remember this. Experiments shouldn't have to be demonstration projects. What's needed is a safe environment where problems can be raised, discussed and worked through.

Disseminating good practice

It's essential to exchange experience. We have come across workers in one part of a social services department unaware of the progress that's been made in another. The problems of communication across services are correspondingly larger. We talked in our introduction of the value of cross-fertilisation. We must share models of good practice as well as develop them. This demands a continuing process of networking, information-exchange and discussion at all levels, within and between agencies and services, between service users and providers, locally, nationally and internationally.

Wider issues

We have seen how agencies can help empower people. But this must be put in context. That context is often *disempowering*. Racism, sexism and other oppressions are endemic in our society. Organisations aren't islands. They reflect these broader problems as well as posing their own. It isn't just a question of awkward agencies, individual customers being ignored, or organisational problems. Whole groups of people are disadvantaged and disempowered. There are widespread economic, political and social inequalities at work. The more that political power is centralised and economic power unequally distributed, the less say people are likely to have.

Recognising this helps us understand the limits of participation. Attempts to empower people which ignore it are likely to be marginal. Sometimes we may feel we are taking on the whole world. To some extent we may be! The participatory initiative we want to take may be small, but the implications of the philosophy underpinning it are enormous. Ultimately participation is concerned with a changed politics, not just changed policies. The conundrum is how far people can get involved to challenge the institutions that disempower them when one of the effects of these institutions is often to limit the extent to which they can be involved.

What we want to emphasise is that trying to increase people's say and involvement is part of this much larger canvas. There are no simple solutions. We inherit all the difficulties and dilemmas with which democracy has struggled for nearly two and a half thousand years. Once we appreciate this, we are likely to make better sense of participation. There are as many models for change as there are political philosophies, from revolution to redistributive social policy. Our small-scale efforts to empower each other don't exist in a separate compartment.

Earlier, we identified three focal points for increasing our say: changing organisations, cultures and climates, and ourselves. Some people emphasise the importance of education and training. We should start learning about our rights and responsibilities as citizens at school. That way we will know how to make use of them and take control of our lives. The first children's rights officer appointed in the United Kingdom wrote to us:

> **'For organisations to bring about fundamental changes of approach and attitude they should concentrate their energies on recruitment and basic training. Good practice is generated by good practitioners and once it becomes endemic it also becomes irresistible.'**

Others stress the importance of legislation. The self-help group of parents with children in care we met felt that hope for the future lay in changes in the law. The law defines our rights and provides a lever to secure them. In Scotland, for example, every local authority is required by law to have an access officer and a positive access policy. The 1986 Disabled Persons Act was similarly seen as a way of improving the rights of disabled people in Britain. American organisations of disabled people long campaigned for anti-discriminatory legislation. In Britain groups are also campaigning for such legislation. One British activist said:

> **'We won't get anything until we get legislation and legislation is going to be difficult to get.'**

People involved in the British disability movement call for an integrated approach to change which points to some of the problems of any one method on its own. One said to us:

> **'We need new paradigms for planning from the bottom up. We can create a framework for change at local and national level with three elements. First, anti-discriminatory legislation. Second, freedom of information, going beyond present legislation, unlocking medical cabinets, banning the keeping of informal files. Third, proper resourcing of disability organisations at both national and local level. You have to see it as an integrated programme. It's possible, but there must be all three elements. With just the first, lawyers will get rich. With the second, there will just be isolated individuals who want to make effective use of it. With only the third, there will be a politically weak movement. With equal opportunities policies and resourcing of organisations at**

local level, you'll have an infra-structure where services could be locally provided.'

Our efforts to increase people's say and involvement will mainly mean taking modest steps at local level. But we should never forget the wider issues involved.

Auditing citizen involvement

If we want to travel along this difficult road of increasing people's say and involvement, we've got to know where we are going. We need directions. Otherwise our efforts to empower may actually be disempowering. To make progress on participation, there must be yardsticks. How else can we make sense of it or know if we are getting it right? We can't define it without them. It's likely to remain vague and confused. We will go on making the same mistakes. Clear criteria are essential if we want to ensure people's involvement, whether we are inspecting, regulating or contracting out services, or trying to democratise our neighbourhoods. Size isn't important. The need is the same for the largest or smallest initiative. Such a checklist will be invaluable in:

● offering a framework for monitoring our own empowerment
● evaluating new and existing services
● untangling the ambiguities of participation
● providing a set of bench marks for new initiatives.

It provides a focus for our reflections, judgements and research.

An instrument for empowerment

With this kind of checklist we can begin to construct an *instrument* for involving and empowering people. It offers a starting point for evaluating participation and developing participatory policy and practice. An instrument for empowerment can help us see what the process and components of a coherent approach to increasing people's say and involvement might look like. It makes it possible to *audit* citizen involvement in a systematic way.

We'd like to make a start in developing such an instrument. Our suggestions follow from the issues raised by our own experience and the many initiatives and schemes we have seen. They are a distillation of the book.

A number of analysts have begun to develop criteria for the assessment of user- or consumer-involvement and control. These include:

- **access** – can consumers obtain the service at all?
- **choice** – is it possible to choose between goods and services on offer, or between those who provide the service?
- **information** – consumers need information in order to judge what serves them best, and the information needs to be expressed in ways which can be understood.
- **redress** – access and choice can be undermined unless consumers can make complaints and receive redress where they do not believe that they have received what they are entitled to.
- **representation** – particularly where there is a monopoly supplier, consumer representation is needed to ensure that the provider of the service doesn't ignore the interests of the consumers.
- **accountability** – are there fair and effective mechanisms for ensuring that service providers are made accountable to those who use services? (National Consumer Council, 1986)

These are helpful, but here we have tried to go further. Readers may feel that's the least we can do after the long and complex journey we've taken them on round participation and empowerment! But to become common currency, such an instrument will need to be developed, refined, tested and agreed. Then it may be really useful. It could help demystify participation, take it out of the realm of the fanciful and exotic and provide some baselines for the future.

An outline instrument

There are three related issues we must take account of in developing such an instrument:

● its own process;
● the process of involvement; and
● key components and dimensions of involvement.

Let's begin with the first of these.

A participatory process of evaluation

The instrument must draw on the views of all interests involved. In personal service, this includes service workers and users, carers, and other local people. It can also offer opportunities for dialogue and exchange by bringing these different perspectives together. As well as feeding into it, participants should be involved in shaping the evaluation. They should have a say in the instrument's formulation and application, and in the collation of its findings. It should be used in a way that equips people to take part in it, for example, by employing trained teams which include service users as well as providers. It should not only mirror a process of empowerment. It could also be part of one. We shouldn't see it as just another technique for researchers. It can be a tool for user and community groups to evaluate the agencies and services they use as well as to help them in their own working.

The process of involvement

An instrument to evaluate people's involvement and empowerment should look at both outcomes and process. They are indivisible. An emphasis on *what* is achieved, to the exclusion of *how*, won't tell us what say or involvement people actually have. If we ignore outcomes and restrict our attention to the provisions of participation, we won't know whether people have really gained anything from it. When we hear what people say about agencies and services, we should put it in context with the information and expectations they have.

Dimensions of involvement

Trying to construct a tool to evaluate participation has reminded us yet again how many facets there are to it. We only have space to headline key dimensions here. At this stage our aim is to chart the landscape rather than to provide detailed measures for all its features. But next to each heading, readers will find page and chapter numbers guiding them to more detailed discussion and breakdowns in the text.

There are also many ways to explore these issues, using a wide repertoire of techniques, including individual interviews and group discussions and both structured and open-ended approaches. Our checklist reflects our particular interest in personal services, but much will be of more general relevance. There must always be flexibility to match particular needs and circumstances. Here then are the dimensions and components of participation which existing initiatives and experience suggest such an instrument will need to explore.

We have identified eight dimensions for evaluating citizen involvement. These are:

Agency objective
Access to the agency
Who is involved
Opportunities and support for involvement
The nature of involvement
Agency practice
Policy for involvement
The effectiveness of involvement.

There are some initial points we should make about these. First, they should all be considered in the light of the prior effect that political, economic and social structures have upon participatory initiatives. These are an important if often unstated element in the equation.

Second, these different dimensions are all in dynamic relation with each other. They can have a profound influence upon each other. For example, an agency which makes it difficult for people to get its services, or which devalues them, is likely to reduce the pool of potential participants in any initiative for involvement. The more positive and productive that people's experience of involvement is, the more people are likely to want to get involved. The more confidence people gain, the more they will press for change in the nature of the agency and for a greater say in it. Change under any one of these headings may help bring about change in another. An obstacle in the way of one may seriously impede others.

Finally, citizen involvement is a complex, sometimes elusive, issue. There are no automatic outcomes. Sometimes initiatives which appear unpromising may lead to more change than those which seem to follow all the rules. For example, a vague commitment to consult may actually achieve more than formal provisions for a say in decision-making – if only because it encourages people to make the most determined efforts to bring about change in an agency. This should not discourage us from approaching citizen involvement in a serious and systematic way, but it is a warning that there are limits to the help we can expect from even the most detailed guidelines and checklists for involvement.

First let's look at what the broad framework looks like schematically and then we will describe it in more detail.

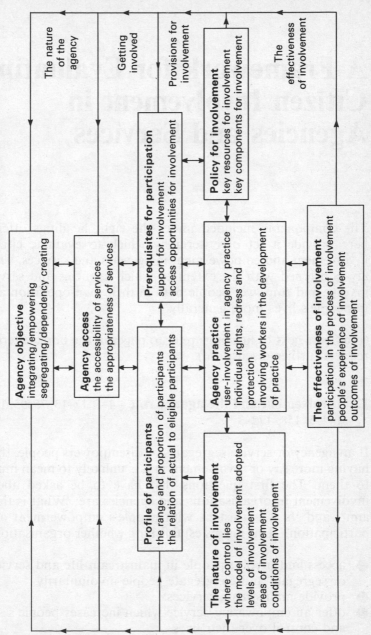

A Framework for Evaluating Citizen Involvement in Agencies and Services

Agency objective
integrating/empowering
segregating/dependency creating

The nature of the agency

Agency access
the accessibility of services
the appropriateness of services

Getting involved

Prerequisites for participation
support for involvement
access opportunities for involvement

Provisions for involvement

Policy for involvement
key resources for involvement
key components for involvement

Profile of participants
the range and proportion of participants
the relation of actual to eligible participants

Agency practice
user-involvement in agency practice
individual rights, redress and protection
involving workers in the development of practice

The effectiveness of involvement
participation in the process of involvement
people's experience of involvement
outcomes of involvement

The effectiveness of involvement

The nature of involvement
where control lies
the model of involvement adopted
levels of involvement
areas of involvement
conditions of involvement

A Framework for Evaluating Citizen Involvement in Agencies and Services

The components included under the eight headings offered here provide a set of criteria by which to evaluate citizen involvement and empowerment in agencies and services. They are concerned with the extent to which agencies and service involve and empower people both in their own operation and in people's lives more generally.

(Numbers next to headings refer to pages in the book offering readers further discussion.)

1. Involvement and the agency role – 4–5, 12–13, 75, 95, 126, 144–5, 158, 172–3

If an agency or service segregates or disempowers people, then having more say or involvement in it is unlikely to mean much to them. The first questions that have to be asked about involvement in organisations and agencies are: 'What is their aim?' and 'Is it consistent with people's empowerment and participation?' This means establishing whether organisations:

- access and involve people in mainstream life and services or segregate and congregate people involuntarily
- provide mainstream services
- offer an empowering service which increases people's say and control over their lives.

2. Access to the agency or service – 74–9, 104–5, 111, 153, 179, 198, 203

Some services are only intended for specific groups, for example women or people who are gay. Others intentionally or otherwise discriminate against use by certain groups, either by restricting their access or by not responding to their particular cultural or ethnic needs. People's opportunities to get involved are minimised if they cannot use the service. Accessible and culturally appropriate services are a prerequisite for people's participation. Criteria to check include:

● whether access is open or for specific groups.
● any restrictions on use according to age, race, class, gender, disability or sexual orientation.
● the sensitivity of agencies and services to people's different needs according to age, race, class, gender, disability or sexuality.
● policy, provisions and monitoring for equal access and opportunities for:

1. workers
2. direct and indirect service users.

● The relation of the **actual** to the **potential** use of the agency or service.

3. The extent of involvement – 6, 13–14, 18–19, 34–7, 39, 52, 79, 104–5, 119–20, 128–30, 138–41, 149–50

There are two key concerns about who becomes involved in participatory initiatives: first, the concern of direct and indirect service users and other local people that arrangements for involvement may exclude or discriminate against some groups; and second, the concern of service providers that the people who get involved may be unrepresentative. This makes the question of who actually gets involved one of the key issues of citizen involvement. Areas to explore include:

the range of potential participants involved
the proportion of potential participants involved
the involvement of people without organisational affiliations
tions
the duration of people's involvement
the relation of participants to the eligible population
according to age, race, gender, sexuality and class
the attitudes and expectations of potential participants to
involvement.

4.   Support and access for people's involvement – 51–2, 108, 150, 192–3

There are two key components which organisations aiming to ensure broad-based involvement should provide to make it possible: **support** and **access**.

Support for involvement – 52–9, 70, 90, 121–3, 165, 195

Without support many people may lack the confidence, skills and resources to participate. This is likely to bias who gets involved. Support has four key components. These are:

personal development – 52–4
practical skills – 54, 67–72, 142–3
practical support – 53–4
support for people to get together and work in groups. – 117–23

Support includes both **personal** and **material support**. Both direct and indirect service users will need it. – 51, 54

Personal support – 56, 137

This includes provision to enhance people's:

self-confidence – 55, 57, 59
assertiveness – 58–9, 146
● self-esteem – 55, 56
expectations – 58, 182
personal development – 52–4

practical skills – 54, 67–72
knowledge and expertise. – 62, 110–12, 141–2, 161–2

Advocacy means speaking on *someone else's* behalf. It is a key form of support for people in dealing with agencies and safeguarding their rights. – 85–6, 88–91

There are four forms of advocacy which offer support in this way:

legal advocacy – 87
professional advocacy – 87–8, 90–1, 164–5
lay or citizen advocacy – 88, 91, 114–15, 162, 169
peer advocacy. – 88

Self-advocacy means speaking *for yourself* and asserting your own rights rather than having someone else speaking for you. Self-advocacy includes speaking and acting for yourself both as an individual and in groups with shared experiences or beliefs.

It includes both: – 56–7, 85, 87, 89–90, 167

(a) individual self-advocacy; and
(b) group self-advocacy.

Support for group self-advocacy – 117–23, 130–43, 154–5, 183
Includes offering opportunities and support for people to:

develop their own accounts – 110–12, 131–2
set up and run their own independent groups and organisations – 121–2, 145–8
learn to work together – 136–7
form their own judgements – 132–4
negotiate decisions and develop demands – 132–3
● take action to achieve change and secure their rights – 87, 137
involve members of minority ethnic communities – 35–6, 105, 139–40, 147
develop specific ethnic minority self-advocacy – 36, 105
● meet and exchange information, ideas and experience with other groups. – 133, 155

Material support – 51, 54

These are the resources which people need if they are to get involved. Without them they would either not be able to take part readily or they would be left out of pocket. They include:

> translation and interpretation – 65–6, 76–7, 104, 141
> respite support – 62
> child care – 62
> appropriate and adequate information – 63–7, 78–9, 96–7, 147, 161–2, 201
> ● travelling and other expenses – 62
> payment for user skills and consultancy – 62
> transport – 195
> meeting places – 62
> ● resources to run their own groups and organisations, including funding for premises, paid workers and running costs. – 62, 141–2

Access for involvement – 15, 79–83, 105–9, 144–8

However well-equipped people are to participate, they also need to have ways into organisations and services if they are to influence what they do and how they are run. Agencies need to provide people with *opportunities* to be involved. This is true whatever kind of involvement is being offered. There are many different ways to provide such opportunities. They may be formal or informal, permanent or temporary, individual or collective. Different forms of involvement may be more or less accessible for different groups. Opportunities for involvement include:

> participation in administrative and political systems – 81, 83, 102
> representation in management structures and forums – 82, 179, 187–8
> access for individual and collective involvement – 32, 171–2
> involvement in direct and representative forums – 150, 183, 186–7
> formal and informal opportunities for involvement – 106, 157

written, verbal and other forms of involvement – 25, 27–8, 31
continuing or one-off opportunities for involvement – 28, 103–4
opportunities for observation. – 171–2

5. The nature of involvement – 8–22

(a) Control of the agency – 3, 9–10, 98, 102, 152–4, 196

There are different approaches, areas and forms for involvement, but perhaps the first question to ask is who actually controls the organisation or service concerned. It's a complex question. Is it the management or shareholders of a commercial service who are in charge? In a state organisation, do the officers, elected members or citizens to whom they are ultimately accountable have the last word? What may be helpful here is to determine whether it is a service led by **services users** or **providers**. This provides a context for understanding the role and nature of people's involvement.

Control lies with:

   service providers
● service purchasers
   direct service users
   indirect service users
   other local people.

(b) Different approaches to involvement – 8–9, 123–4, 179–80

There are two different, sometimes conflicting, models and philosophies of citizen involvement: the consumerist and democratic approaches.They are associated with different ways of involving people: consumerism with information-gathering and consultation; the democratic approach with people having a direct say in decision-making. Each has its strengths and weaknesses. It is helpful to distinguish between them.

The forms of involvement employed: – 93–4

(a) information gathering – 23–4 }
(b) consultation – 24   } Chapter 2 (23–41), 42–8
(c) direct say in decision-making. – Chapter 3 (42–59), 79,
      170–1

(c) Levels of involvement – 10–12, 15–16, 198–200

There are three key levels for people's involvement: personal,
organisational and developmental. These correspond to three
related settings for their intervention. They are:

(a) in people's personal dealings with agencies and services
(b) in running and managing agencies and services
(c) in planning and developing new policies, organisations
      and services.

(d) Areas of involvement

There are a wide range of areas for people's involvement in
agencies and service provision. These include involvement in:

   expenditure and budgetary control – 67, 179–80
   recruitment – 68
   training – 69
   standard-setting – 187–8, 194–5
   quality-assurance – 187–8, 194–5
   inspection – 103
 ● designing and placing contracts – 180
   monitoring and evaluation – 72–4, 98–9, 183, 188, 195
   providing services – 152–4
   designing and controlling individual support schemes. –
   11–12, 152–3

(e) Conditions of involvement – 96–102, 123–7, 191

Agencies will not always be able to respond to what people
want. They may have to reconcile the competing interests of
different groups. But they will need to agree and make clear

the conditions of people's involvement and what they can expect from getting involved. This raises three issues:

the terms of involvement
agency commitments to citizen involvement
safeguards for people's participation.

6. Agency practice – Chapter 8 (157–76)

Participatory practice is the starting point for people's involvement in agencies. It means that people have a say in the practice they receive from agency workers and that a central objective of practice is increasing the say and involvement they have in their lives. Participatory practice makes possible a more equal instead of a dependent relationship between service users and workers, challenges artificial barriers between them and makes for a way of working that is supportive instead of directive. It has three key elements:

● user involvement in practice – 158–65
ensuring individual rights, redress and protection – 165–71, 174–5
the involvement of workers in the development of practice. – 190–1

(a) User-involvement in practice – 157–63, 170–1, 175

User-involvement in agency practice is concerned with people having a say both in what happens to them and in their relationship with workers. It includes the involvement of service users in individual:

‾ assessment/defining their own needs – 110–12
planning – 170–1
recording – 167–70
action – 79, 172–3
review. – 58, 175

214   *Citizen Involvement*

It also includes:

>   an agreed and published code of practice – 160
>   choice of service and practitioner – 160
> ● full and appropriate information, interpreting and trans-
>   lated materials – 63–7, 76–9
>   accessible and positive language – 75–7, 84–5, 168–9
>   positive imaging of service users – 160
>   the employment of people with direct experience of
>   services as service users. – 71–2, 193–4

(b) Individual rights, redress and protection

There are three essential ways in which people's rights should
be safeguarded in services: – 12, 14–15, 165–71, 174–5, 201

>   effective complaints procedure – 43, 165–6
>   data protection – 167
>   access to records. – 167–70, 184–6, 199–200

(c) Participatory practice and the involvement of workers – 157,
   175–6

The involvement of workers in the development of participatory practice will help ensure both that it is workable and that
it is actually adopted. Three key components will support this:

>   workers' rights agreed and protected – 110, 154, 173–4
>   support for staff to work in a participatory way – 157, 175–
>   6, 187
>   staff involvement in developing participatory provisions
>   and practice. – 109–10, 175–6, 189–90, 202

7.   Agency policy for involvement – Chapter 9 (177–220),
   39–40

Coherent policies are required for the development of effective initiatives for citizen involvement. A series of key
resources and components underpin these.

(a) Agency resources for involvement – Chapter 4 (60–91)

Finance: to support user involvement – 18, 61, 63
Training: for both service providers and service users – 67–72, 185
Information: for informed choice and decisions – 36, 46, 63–7, 96–7, 161–2, 201
Advocacy: including citizen, professional and self-advocacy, to ensure people have an effective voice – 56–7, 85–91, 114–15, 164–5
Monitoring and evaluation: to establish outcomes and extend knowledge and understanding – 40, 72–4, 200, 217
Equal access and opportunities: to ensure appropriate services reach all communities – 74–9, 104–5, 111
Time: to enable involvement to develop – 61, 136
Appropriate forms and structures for involvement: to make possible broad-based and anti-discriminatory involvement – 68, 79–83, 105–9, 128–30
The dissemination of good practice: to share and build on what is already known. – 197

(b) Components for an effective policy for involvement – 101–2, 107–8, 178–89

Clear agency/project goals and values
Key people, groups or bodies inside the agency dedicated to the initiative and carrying it forward
Gaining widespread support for involvement within the organisation
An emphasis on citizen involvement in recruitment, training and promotion
Funding conditional upon people's involvement
Earmarked budgets to increase people's say and involvement
Agency users' involvement in the formulation and planning of participatory initiatives
Participatory management systems
Development projects which feed into mainstream agency policy and practice, diffusing as well as demonstrating ideas
A source of independent skills for training and development
Continuous monitoring and evaluation.

8.   The effectiveness of involvement – 40, 124-7

Efforts to involve people run the risk of becoming an end in themselves. While being involved can bring its own benefits – giving people a chance to say things they have never been able to say before, or to be heard when no one has previously ever asked them what they thought – this is not enough. The acid test of initiatives to involve people is: **how much participants are themselves involved in shaping them; how participants experience them**; and **what initiatives actually achieve**.

(a) A participatory process of involvement – 32-4, 40-1, 94-6, 98-9, 177-8, 183-4, 192, 202

The most effective initiatives and strategies for citizen involvement seem to be those which people are themselves involved in shaping from the start. Citizen involvement demands a participatory process as well as participatory objectives. The two are inextricable. Issues to examine include:

> who the initiative comes from, including direct and indirect service users, other local people, service purchasers and providers
> stages at which participants are involved
> ● the interests involved in the development of participatory initiatives, including service workers, direct and indirect service users and other local people
> a published programme widely available including the objectives and timescale of the initiative
> opportunities and support for the exchange and negotiation of the different and competing interests involved
> provisions for decisions and demands to feed into the agency structure
> reporting back to participants
> implementing action
> time scale for achieving change
> findings of monitoring publicly available.

(b) People's experience of involvement – 16–17, 19–20, 52–3, 73, 145–7, 155, 186, 202

There are likely to be many different perspectives on the effectiveness of efforts to involve people. Agencies will have their own ideas and criteria. But the views of actual and potential participants have a particular importance because *their* involvement is the object of the exercise. Such views include:

● attitudes to the agency or service
● awareness and understanding of opportunities for involvement
● attitudes to provisions and methods of participation
● views of outcomes
● views of people who do not get involved.

(c) The outcomes of involvement – 100, 111, 155, 194, 217

The relationship between people's involvement and change may not be straightforward. Instead of taking it for granted we should examine it more closely. How does it actually work? It is also helpful to look at both agency/service outcomes and outcomes for agency/service users. Attention should not be restricted to change in the agency or service, although this is clearly important. It is also important to consider what if any improvements there are more generally in people's lives. There are three dimensions to explore:

1. The relationship between people's involvement and change
2. Agency/service outcomes – improvements in:

accessibility
acceptability
flexibility
reliability

choice
sufficiency
coordination (Huxley and others, 1990; Ramcharan and others, 1990).

3.   Outcomes for agency/service users:

increased opportunities for personal growth and development
improved quality of life
increased social integration
equality of outcomes according to race, class, gender, age, disability and sexual orientation.

Using the instrument

Last, some words of warning. We should always be aware of the limitations of such a tool. It's intended as an aid, not a straitjacket. Our efforts to empower ourselves and other people will often fall short of the ideal. An instrument's value is in signposting the route, not giving a precise destination or telling us we have failed to arrive.

We shouldn't use it mechanically. It's unlikely to reflect all the issues and subtleties of participation. Many of the dimensions we want to explore won't be readily quantifiable. Empowerment can't be reduced to a set of boxes which we can tick off. We should be sceptical of any approach that suggests it can.

We have talked about the importance of evaluation. But it's not an automatic choice for many people. One researcher said to us

'It's expensive to do good research and hard to convince senior managers that it's worth it. Not much pay off is seen for evaluation measures.'

This kind of instrument can facilitate research and evaluation, but we must still expect to meet resistance to them.

It's not enough to base it on crude indicators like, 'Is there a users' group?', 'Do you have a complaints procedure?', 'Can people be present at meetings?', 'Is information available for people using a service?' Increasing people's say and involvement can't be reduced to another set of procedures. As we have seen, such paper rights may count for little or nothing. We need to know what they actually mean for people.

Finally, as we have already suggested, we shouldn't assume there are direct links between people's participation and change. One development worker said:

'It won't always be clear if there is a simple and straightforward causal connection between people being involved and something happening. We don't know whether it coincidentally fits in with what somebody in authority has already begun to feel they might want to do; whether our voice has merely reinforced one of the prevailing opinions and it is only for that reason it has gone ahead. This isn't to say that you can never know whether it's been worth it or if it works, but that it may not always be as it seems and that the effects of involvement may be subtle and difficult to measure.'

Conclusion

We have talked of increasing people's say and involvement as a journey. It's an exciting journey and one of the most important to make. It's difficult to see how organisations and services which don't embark on it can avoid being disabling. But it certainly isn't easy. We hope this doesn't frighten people off. Hopefully we've pointed out some of the pitfalls and provided some more signposts.

There are two things we have wanted to do in this book, because they are so rarely done. The first is to put participation and empowerment in a political and a personal context. The second is to offer practical ways forward from the wide range of experience that already exists.

What's special for us about empowerment is that it's both a means and an end. As agencies offer and people gain more say and involvement, democracy starts to become a reality in our day-to-day life. We come to recognise, want and expect it. We learn how to achieve it. Each agency we have more say in makes it possible for us to take greater control over our lives. Each change we make provides the basis for another. Every organisation that becomes more accountable, brings us nearer to changing the world we live in.

It's a journey that's both far-reaching and small-scale. It isn't the bloody revolution which promises to change everything and leaves us excluded just the same. It isn't the prescriptive policy that's meant to improve our lot, but stigmatises and makes us dependent. It doesn't mean we must make giant strides. There's probably something wrong if we are trying to. We don't have to feel guilty about the modesty of our progress. The smallest steps will take us forward, so long as we keep heading in the right direction. Our final goal may still seem light years away. As one person, long working to increase people's say and involvement, said: 'Many changes that are starting now, I won't see happen in my lifetime'. But we will make gains. Some people's lives are already being changed. We will see differences.

Further Reading

Addison, C. (1988) *Planning Investigative Projects: A Workbook for Social Services Practitioners*, London, Practice and Development Exchange, National Institute for Social Work.

Arnstein, S. (1969) 'A ladder of citizen participation in the USA', *Journal of the American Institute Of Planners*, 35, 4, 216–24.

Baker, P. (1989) 'Talking the client's language', *Social Work Today*, 23 March, 24–5.

Baker. P., Hussain, Z. and Saunders, J. (1991) *Interpreters in Public Service*, Birmingham, Venture Press.

Barclay, P.M. (1982) (The Barclay Report) *Social Workers: Their Role and Tasks*, London, Bedford Square Press.

Barker, I. (1991) 'Agents for Change', *Open Mind*, no. 53.

Barker, I. and Peck, E. (eds) (1987) *Power in Strange Places: User Empowerment in Mental Health Services*, London, Good Practices in Mental Health.

Barnes, C. (1991) *Disabled People in Britain and Discrimination: A Case for Anti-Discrimination Legislation*, London, Hurst & Co. in association with the British Council of Organisations of Disabled People.

Beeforth, M., Conlan, E., Field, V., Hoser, B. and Sayce, L. (eds) (1990) *Whose Service Is It Anyway?: User Views on Coordinating Community Care*, London, Research and Development for Psychiatry.

Beresford, P. (1982) 'Public participation and the redefinition of social policy', in Jones, C. and Stevenson, J. (eds), *The Year Book of Social Policy in Britain 1980–81*, London, Routledge & Kegan Paul.

Beresford, P. and Croft, S. (1978) *A Say in the Future: Planning, Participation and Meeting Social Need*, London, Battersea Community Action.

221

Beresford, P. and Croft, S. (1986) *Whose Welfare: Private Care or Public Services?*, Brighton, Lewis Cohen Urban Studies Centre.

Berry, L. and Doyle, N. (1988) *Open to Complaints: Guidelines for Social Services Complaints Procedures*, London, National Consumer Council/National Institute for Social Work.

Boaden, N., Goldsmith, M., Hampton, W., and Stringer, P. (1982) *Public Participation in Local Services*, Harlow, Longman.

Brandon, A. and D. (1987) *Consumers as Colleagues*, London, MIND.

Brandon, D. (1981) *Voices of Experience: Consumer Perspectives of Psychiatric Treatment*, London, MIND.

Brandon, D. (1991) *Innovation Without Change*, London, Macmillan.

Brandon, D. and A. (1988) *Putting People First: A Handbook on the Practical Application of Ordinary Living Principles*, London, Good Impressions Publishing.

Brandon, D. and Towe, N. (1989) *Free To Choose: An Introduction to Service Brokerage* (Community Living Monograph) London, Good Impressions Publishing.

Brechin, A. and Swain, J. (1986) *Changing Relationships: Shared Action Planning with People with a Mental Handicap*, London, Harper & Row.

Butler, K., Carr , S. and Sullivan, F. (1988) *Citizen Advocacy: A Powerful Partnership*, London, National Citizen Advocacy.

Chamberlin, J. (1988) *On Our Own: Patient-Controlled Alternatives to the Mental Health System*, London, MIND.

Coalition, The official magazine of the Greater Manchester Coalition of Disabled People, Manchester.

Community Care (1989) *User involvement*, Inside Supplement, *Community Care*, London, 27 April.

Community Care (1992) *Involving Service Users*, inside supplement, *Community Care*, London, 26 March.

Community Development Journal (1988) Consumer action and community development issue, *Community Development Journal*, 23, 4, Oxford University Press.

Connelly, N. (1985) *Social Services Departments and Race: A Discussion Paper*, Discussion Paper No. 12, London, Policy Studies Institute.

Connelly, N. (1989) *Race And Change In Social Services Departments,* London, Policy Studies Institute.

Connelly, N. (1990) *Raising Voices: Social Services Departments and People with Disabilities*, London, Policy Studies Institute.

Cooper, D. and Hersov, J. (1988) *We Can Change the Future: Self-Advocacy for People with Learning Difficulties – A Staff Training*

Resource (book and video) London, National Bureau for Students with Disabilities.

Corby, B. (1987) Why ignoring the rights of parents in child abuse cases should be avoided, *Social Work Today*, 23 November, 8–9.

Cornwell, J. (1990) *The Consumers' View: Elderly People and Community Health Services*, London, King's Fund Centre.

Crawley, B.(1988) *The Growing Voice: A Survey of Self-Advocacy Groups in Adult Training Centres and Hospitals in Great Britain*, London, Values Into Action.

Crawley, B., Mills, J., Wertheimer, A., Whittaker, A., Williams, P. and Billis, J. (1988) *Learning About Self-Advocacy*, London, Values Into Action.

Crewe, N.M. and Zola, I.K. (1983) *Independent Living for Physically Disabled People*, London, Jossey-Bass.

Croft, S. and Beresford, P. (1984) 'Patch and participation: the case for citizen research', *Social Work Today*, 17 September, 18–24.

Croft, S. and Beresford, P. (1989) User involvement, citizenship and social policy, *Critical Social Policy*, 26, 5–18.

Croft, S. and Beresford, P. (1990) *From Paternalism to Participation: Involving People in Social Services*, London, Open Services Project/Joseph Rowntree Foundation.

Dennis, N. (1970) *People and Planning: The Sociology of Housing in Sunderland*, London, Faber & Faber.

Dennis, N. (1972) *Public Participation and Planners' Blight*, London, Faber & Faber.

Dowson, S. (1990) *Keeping It Safe: Self-Advocacy by People with Learning Difficulties and the Professional Response*, London, Values Into Action.

Dowson, S. (1991) *Moving to the Dance: Or Service Culture and Community Care*, London, Values Into Action.

Dutt, R. (1990) Community care and black people, *Community Care* supplement, NCVO News, National Council for Voluntary Organisations, January/February.

Eurosocial (1987) *Client Access to Personal Social Services Records*, Eurosocial Report No. 30, Vienna.

Finlay, R. and Reynolds, J. (1987) *Social Work and Refugees: A Handbook on Working with People in Exile in the UK*, Derby, National Extension College/Refugee Action.

Fisher, M. (ed.) (1983) *Speaking of Clients,* Sheffield, University of Sheffield/*Community Care*.

Gardner, R. (1987) *Who Says: Choice and Control in Care*, London, National Children's Bureau.

Genn, H. and Genn, Y. (1989) *The Effectiveness of Representation at Tribunals*, London, Lord Chancellor's Department.

Good Practices in Mental Health (1986) *Advocacy Information Pack*, London Good Practices in Mental Health.

Griffiths, R. (1988) (Griffiths Report) *Community Care: Agenda for Action*, London, HMSO.

Hallet, C. (1987) *Critical Issues in Participation*, Newcastle-upon-Tyne, Association of Community Workers.

Hampshire Centre for Independent Living (1986) *One Step On*, Petersfield, Hampshire Centre for Independent Living.

Hampshire Centre for Independent Living (1986) *Source Book Towards Independent Living*, Petersfield, Hampshire Centre for Independent Living.

Hampshire Centre for Independent Living (1990) Papers on independent living, consumer consultation, assessment, meeting assistance needs, respite care and day centres, Petersfield, Hampshire Centre for Independent Living.

Hevey, D. (1992) *The Creatures Time Forgot: Photography and Disability Imagery*, London, Routledge & Kegan Paul.

Hodgson, D. (1992) *Children's Participation in Social Work Planning – Practical Pointers from the Experiences of Young People and Social Workers*, London, National Children's Bureau.

Hodgson, D. (1992) *Children's Participation Pack, London, National Children's Bureau.*

Hoggett, P. and Hambleton, R. (1987) *Decentralisation and Democracy: Localising Public Services*, Occasional paper No. 28, Bristol, School of Advanced Urban Studies, University of Bristol.

Hunter, E. (1990) 'The right stuff', *Social Work Today*, 24 May, 16–17.

Hutchison, M., Linton, G. and Lucas, J. (1990) *User Involvement Inform-ation Pack: From Policy to Practice*, London, MIND South-East.

Huxley, P., Hagan, T., Hennelly, R. and Hunt, J. (1990) *Effective Community Mental Health Services*, Aldershot, Avebury.

Hyde-Price, C. (1986) *Our Users' Voice: The Effect of Patient Opinion Surveys on the Management of the Health Service*, London, Report prepared for the National Management Trainee Scheme.

Kettleborough, H. (1988) 'Consulting women in the community about local government services', *Critical Social Policy,* Issue 21, Spring, 56–7.

Kingsley, S. (1985) *Action-Research: Method or Ideology*, Association of Researchers into Voluntary Action and Community Involvement, Occasional paper No.8, Wivenhoe, Essex, ARVAC.

Kocher, P. (1989) *Information and Advice Project*, Lewes, Age Concern, East Sussex.

Lister, R. (1990) *The Exclusive Society: Citizenship and the Poor*, London, Child Poverty Action Group.

Lister, R. and Beresford, P. (1991) *Working Together Against Poverty: Involving Poor People in Action Against Poverty*, London, Open Services Project/Department of Applied Social Studies, University of Bradford.

Local Government Management Board (1987) *Getting Closer to the Public*, Luton, Local Government Management Board.

Local Government Management Board (1989) *Learning from the Public*, Luton, Local Government Management Board.

Mansbridge, J.J. (1983) *Beyond Adversary Democracy*, Chicago, University of Chicago Press.

Mantle, A. (1985) *Popular Planning Not in Practice: Confessions of a Community Worker*, London, Greenwich Employment Unit.

McDonald, A. (1986) *The Weller Way: The Story of the Weller Streets Housing Co-operative*, London, Faber & Faber.

Millner, L. Ash, A. and Ritchie, P. (1991) *Quality in Action: A Resource Pack for Improving Services for People with Learning Difficulties*, Bristol, Norah Fry Research Centre, University of Bristol.

Morris, J. (1991) *Pride Against Prejudice – Transforming Attitudes to Disability*, London, Women's Press.

National Consumer Council (1982) *Consumer Concerns Survey*, London, National Consumer Council.

National Consumer Council (1986), *Measuring Up: Consumer Assessment of Local Authority Services, a Guideline Study*, London, National Consumer Council.

National Council for Voluntary Organisations (1984) *Clients Rights,* Report of an NCVO Working Party, London, Bedford Square Press/NCVO.

Oakley, A. (1981) 'Interviewing women: a contradiction in terms', in Helen Roberts (ed.), *Doing Feminist Research*, London, Routledge & Kegan Paul) 30–61.

O'Brien, J. and Tyne, A. (1981) *The Principle of Normalisation – A Foundation for Effective Services*, London, Values Into Action.

O'Brien, J. (1987) *Learning from Citizen Advocacy Programs*, Georgia, USA, Georgia Advocacy Office.

O'Brien, J. and Lyle, C. (1987) *Framework for Accomplishment: A Workshop for People Developing Better Services,* Georgia, USA, Responsive Systems Associates.

O'Hagan, B. (1987) 'Efficiency, enrichment and empowerment', *Journal of Community Education*, 6, 1, 2–5.

O'Hagan, M. (1992) *Stopovers on My Way Home from Mars: A Winston Churchill Fellowship Report on the Psychiatric Survivor*

Movement in the USA, Britain and The Netherlands, Survivors Speak Out.

Oliver, M. (1987) 'Re-defining disability: a challenge to research', *Research Policy and Planning*, 5, 1, 9–13.

Oliver, M. (1990) *The Politics of Disablement*, London, Macmillan.

Oliver, M. (1992), Review of Connelly, N., 'Raising voices: social services departments and people with disabilities', *Critical Social Policy*, 33, Winter 1991/92, 115–16.

Oliver, M. and Zarb, G. (1989) 'The politics of disability: a new approach', *Disability, Handicap and Society*, 4, 3, 221–39.

Otto, S. and Armstrong, F. (1978) *The Action Research Experiment: A Report of Two Years Work by the Consortium Action Research Team 1975–1977*, London, South East London Consortium.

Ouseley, H. (1985) '"Treating them all the same": decentralising institutionalised racism', *Going Local?*, Polytechnic of Central London, April, 8–9.

Ovretveit, J. (1986) *Improving Social Work Records and Practice: Report of the BASW/BIOSS Action Research Project into Social Work Recording and Client Participation*, Birmingham, British Association of Social Workers.

Pagel, M. (1988) *On Our Own Behalf: An Introduction to the Self-Organisation of Disabled People*, Manchester, Greater Manchester Coalition of Disabled People.

Ramcharan, P., Grant, G. and McGrath, M. (1990) 'Reconciling value-directed and value-relative approaches to evaluation research: the case of the service packaging project', Working paper, Bangor, Centre for Social Policy Research and Development, University College of North Wales.

Reason, P. and Rowan, J. (eds) (1981) *Human Inquiry: A Source Book of New Paradigm Research*, Chichester, John Wiley.

Richardson, A. (1983) *Participation*, Concepts In Social Policy, 1, London, Routledge & Kegan Paul.

Roberts, H. (ed.) (1981) *Doing Feminist Research*, London, Routledge & Kegan Paul.

Rose, S.M. and Black, B.L. (1986) *Advocacy and Empowerment: Mental Health Care in the Community*, Boston, Mass., Routledge & Kegan Paul.

Sang, B. and O'Brien, J. (1984) 'Advocacy: the UK and American experiences', King's Fund Project Paper No. 51, London, King's Fund Centre.

Scott-Parker, S. (1989) *They Aren't in the Brief: Advertising People with Disabilities*, London, King's Fund Centre.

Shearer, A. (1986) *Building Community with People with Mental*

Handicaps, Their Families and Friends, London, Campaign for Mentally Handicapped People and King's Fund Centre.

Shearer, A. (1991) *Who Calls the Shots: Public Services and How They Serve the People Who Use Them*, London, King's Fund Centre.

Shemmings, D. (1991) *Client Access to Records: Participation in Social Work*, Aldershot, Avebury Gower.

Shemmings, D. (1991) *Family Participation In Child Protection Conferences In Lewisham Social Services*, Norwich, University of East Anglia.

Shemmings, D. and Thoburn, J. (1990) *Parental Participation in Child Protection Conferences: Report of a Pilot Project in Hackney Social Services Department*, Norwich, Social Work Development Unit, University of East Anglia.

Stanton, A. (1989) *Invitation to Self-Management*, Ruislip, Dab Hand Press.

Survivors Speak Out (1988) *Self-Advocacy Action Pack: Empowering Mental Health Service Users*, London, Survivors Speak Out.

Tester, S. and Meredith, B. (1987) *Ill-Informed: A Study of Information and Support for Elderly People in the Inner City*, London, Policy Studies Institute.

Thompson, C. (ed.) (1991) *Changing The Balance: Power and People Who Use Services*, London, Community Care Project, National Council for Voluntary Organisations.

Thompson, J. (1985) *Community Architecture: The Story of Lea View House, Hackney*, London, Royal Institute of British Architects Community Architecture Group.

Thompson, P. (1978) *The Voice Of The Past*, Oxford University Press.

Trevillion, S. (1992) *Caring in the Community: A Networking Approach to Community Partnership*, London, Longmans.

Tyne, A. (1987) *Keeping Up To The "PASS" Mark: Evaluation of Community Services*, Community Living, November/December.

Wagner, G. (1988) (The Wagner Report) *Residential Care: A Positive Choice*, London, National Institute for Social Work/HMSO.

Wates, N. and Knevitt, C. (1987) *Community Architecture: How People Are Creating The Own Environment*, Harmondsworth, Penguin Books.

Wertheimer, A. (1988). *Self-Advocacy Skills Training: Report of Two Workshops Held Between April and September 1987*, London, The King's Fund Centre.

Wertheimer, A. (1989). *Making Our Voice Heard: Strengthening Alliances Between People Who Use Services*, London, Kings Fund Centre.

White, I., Devenney, M., Bhaduri, R., Beresford, P., Barnes, J., and Jones, A. (1988). *Hearing the Voice of the Consumer*, London, Policy Studies Institute.

Whittaker, A. (1990) 'Involving people with learning difficulties in meetings', in Winn, L. (ed.), *Power to the People: The Key to Responsive Services in Health and Social Care*, London, King's Fund Centre.

Whittaker, A., Gardner, S. and Kershaw, J. (1991) *Service Evaluation by People with Learning Difficulties*, London, King's Fund Centre.

Whittaker, A. (ed.) (1991) *Supporting Self-Advocacy*, London, King's Fund Centre.

Williams, P. and Shoultz, B. (1982) *We Can Speak for Ourselves: Self-Advocacy by Mentally Handicapped People*, Human Horizons Series, London, Souvenir Press.

Winn, L. (ed.) (1990) *Power to the People: The Key to Responsive Services in Health and SocialCare*, London, Kings Fund Centre.

Wood, R. (1988) 'Disabled people point the way forward', *Social Work Today*, 21 January, 16–17.

Wood, R. (1991) *Speak Up for Yourself: Putting Advocacy into Practice*, London, Age Concern England.

Wright, M. (1988) *A Sense Of History: Reminiscence Work with Elderly People*, London, Lewisham Social Services.

Index

access
  for involvement 51–2, 150,
    201, 205–7, 210
  physical 75, 99
  to records 167–70, 184–6
accessibility
  advocacy 89
  information-gathering and
    consultation 39
accountability 201
accounts, developing 131–2
actual say 52
actual use of agencies 206
advisers 121–3, 161
advisory panels 28, 45, 47
advocacy 85–91, 209
  collective action 114
  reminiscence work 112
  rights 169
agency access 205, 206–7
agency forums 143–4, 147
agency objectives 204–6
agency practice 205–6, 213–15
agendas
  information-gathering and
    consultation 44, 45–6
  involvement of 126–7
  judgement forming 133
  personal 33
air-time 23
alliances 176

allies 80, 123
analysis
  information-gathering and
    consultation 38
  of involvement 48
anti-racism strategies 105, 194
apathy 43
apprenticing of
  newcomers 138
approaches to
  involvement 211
areas of involvement 10–13,
  212
assertiveness 56, 57, 59, 146
assumptions and
  consultation 32
attitudes, changing 194
auditing involvement 200
awareness of rights 165

Barclay Report 43
bias 52, 106
  information-gathering and
    consultation 34–7
black people 4, 6, 140
  provision for 104–5
  racial harassment 110
  secure accommodation 145
  training 68
  see also ethnic minorities,
    members of

bottom-up initiatives 2, 190–2, 199
broad-based
    involvement 139–41
budgeting 18
    devolved 179–80
    training 67
businesses and involvement
    policy 178–80

campaigning 15, 16
care, young people in
    forums 82–3, 147–8
    magazine 112
    scepticism 98
    self-confidence 57
care services 5
carers
    guidelines for 154
    minority ethnic
        communities 35–6
    support for 62
case/care management 87–8
challenges to
    empowerment 171–5
change, checklist for 127
checklists
    for change 127
    for information-gathering and
        consultation 41
    for involvement 179, 200,
        205–19
child protection 170–1, 172,
    174
childcare
    collective action 115
    forums 82–3
    legislation 174–5
children
    in care 159, 166, 170–1
    disabled 92
    families with 13
    with HIV 167
    involvement of 79

    with learning difficulties 92
    rights of 168, 174–5
    see also young people
Children Act (1989) 79
choice of involvement 3,
    108–9, 201
citizen advocacy 88, 89, 91,
    162, 209
citizen forums 143
citizenship issues 4–6
claimant's commission 62
climate change 16
co-counselling 152
coalitions 153, 183–4
collaboration 118
collation of information 38, 39
collective action 113–27
collective advocacy 88
collective discussions see
    group discussions
collectives 81
commitment to
    involvement 97–100
communication
    of experience 197
    limits of 42–3
    see also interaction
community care
    strategy 190–1
community development
    117–20, 181–2
    approach to 37
    guidelines for 120–1
    pressures on 192
    skills for 15
community education 48
community groups 15, 66
community orientation 3, 118
community participation 3, 4
community presence 3
community profiling 24
competence
    advocacy 89
    improvement of 3

complaints procedures 165–6, 176, 188
components for involvement 215
conditional involvement 212–13
access to resources 109
training 68, 69
conditioning 68, 69
conferences *see* search conferences
confidence-building 55–7, 101
advocacy 122
judgement forming 133
confidentiality
and advisers 122
rights 167, 168
conflicting interests 14
confrontation 118
consideration and involvement 107
consultants 137, 177–8
consultation 23, 24–30, 37–41
agency decisions 94, 98
guidelines for 30–7
minority ethnic communities 104
responsiveness to 42–9
consumer advisory panels 28, 45, 47
consumerism 8–9, 109, 179–80, 211–12
community development 124
complaints procedures 165
information-gathering and consultation 49–50, 51
language 85
limitations of 14
quality control 194
continuity of involvement 103–4
continuous sampling 28

control
of agencies 211
environments 173
and responsibility 9–10
costs
of information-gathering and consultation 38
of involvement 18, 19, 61
council tenants 7–8
counselling 158
courtesy, importance of 33–4, 40
credibility of participants 111–12
criticism, attitudes towards 197
culture change 16

data protection 167
day centres 95, 139
decentralisation 3, 6, 75
decision-making process 170–1, 183
democratic model 9, 20
information-gathering and consultation 49
involvement policy 211–12, 219–20
dependency 172–3
desire for involvement 20–2
determined advocacy 90
development
of accounts 131–2
community *see* community development
involvement in 11
of involvement policy 177–89
of training 71–2
devolved budgets 179–80
dialogue 26
'difficult people', dealing with 137

dimensions of
    involvement   203–4
direct action   116
direct say   49–50, 94
disabled people   9, 92, 140,
    183–4
  advocacy   89, 90
  citizenship   4–6
  collective action   115, 116
  empowerment of   129–30,
    133, 138, 139
  equal opportunities   75, 78–9
  forums   80, 83, 144, 146,
    147
  identity   151, 152
  negotiation   135
  politics   3, 199–200
  relating to   193
  representation of   150
  research by   74
  safeguards for   99
  self-confidence of   56
  self-operated support
    schemes   10, 152, 153–4
  sensory disabilities   76, 78–9
  social services   13
  support for   53–4, 66, 67,
    123, 196
  survey of   107
  training of   71–2
Disabled Persons Act
    (1986)   89, 199
discrimination
  agencies   207
  empowerment   149
  information-gathering and
    consultation   34–7
  involvement   106, 108
discussions   31–2
  see also group discussions
distrust and participation   43

education and
    involvement   198–9

effectiveness
  of information-gathering and
    consultation   29–37
  of involvement   205, 216–18
effects
  of information   38–40, 43–4
  of involvement   1–2, 21
efficiency
  of information-gathering and
    consultation   48
  of involvement   17–18
effort and consultation   37–8
employment obligations   4
empowerment   128–36
  community
    development   124
  development of   157–60
  forums for   143–8
  guidelines for   154–5
  information-gathering and
    consultation   48, 49–52
  instrument for   202–19
  issues   141–3
  method of   61
  pressure against   148–9,
    171–5
  principles for   160–3
  requirements for   65, 85
  and rights   164–71
  support for   175–6
  therapeutic benefits of   109
enabling involvement   54–5,
    120, 130, 138–41
enrichment in information-
    gathering and
    consultation   48, 49
equal access and
    opportunities   74–9, 82
  employment policies   194
  minority ethnic
    communities   105
  training   68, 70
equal rights   4, 5
ethics groups   188

ethnic minorities, members of
  citizenship qualification 4
  collective action 116
  discrimination 153
  enabling involvement 140
  equal opportunities 75, 76–7
  information-gathering and
    consultation 35–6
  provision for 104–5
  see also black people
evaluation
  of consultation 104
  of involvement 72–4, 103,
    202, 217
  of standards 194–5
exchanges 163, 197
exclusions
  information-gathering and
    consultation 34–7
  involvement 106
exhibitions 25
expectations and
    involvement 54, 56, 58
experiences of
    involvement 217
expert information 67
expertise and
    consultation 37–8
experts, working with 142–3
exploitation 125

familiarity and
    involvement 107
families with children 13, 168
  see also parents
feedback 26, 28, 34, 40
feminists
  information-gathering and
    consultation 37
  language 84
  research discussions 47
flexibility of
    involvement 107–8, 195–6
focus groups 27–8, 44

focusing of discussions 31
formal advocacy 88
formal say 52
formality
  of accounts 132
  and involvement 106–7, 147
forms for involvement 105–7
forums 79–83, 104, 105–7
  for empowerment 143–8
framework for
    involvement 205
freedom, restriction of 13–14
funding 184, 187
  see also grants

goals for change 100–1
grants
  community
    development 118
  equal opportunities 105
Griffiths Report 43
group discussions
  effectiveness of 47
  example 29–30
  information-gathering and
    consultation 27, 32, 33
group work 13–14, 15
guidelines
  community
    development 120–1
  empowerment 154–5
  information-gathering and
    consultation 30–7

health service 62–3, 64
help and consultation 32–3
history of involvement 6–7
HIV *see* people with
    HIV/AIDS
homeless people
  empowerment of 159–60
  relating to 193
  self-confidence of 58
honesty 121, 174

housing groups 65, 117
see also tenants
human rights 164

identity 151–2
image of agencies 27
importance of
involvement 19–20
imposition of
participation 189–90
independence
advisers 121
advocacy 89, 164
service culture 4
individual action 113–15,
116–17
individual discussions 32
inefficiency see efficiency
inertia 43
informal advocacy 88
informality
of accounts 132
and involvement 106–7, 147
information
for involvement 63–7, 183,
201
judgement forming 133
information-gathering 23–4,
25–30, 37–41
agency decisions 94, 98
guidelines 30–7
responsiveness 42–9
informing people 161–2
initiatives, participatory 15,
39–41, 52, 56
instrument for
empowerment 202–19
integrated
accommodation 154, 184,
192
integrated approach to
change 199–200
integration of
involvement 101–2

interaction
consultation 25, 26
judgement forming 133
see also communication
interest in involvement 2–4
interests 3
interpreters
equal opportunities 76–7
information-gathering and
consultation 35–6
intervention between
citizens 14–15

joint monitoring 195
joint training 70–1
judgements, formation
of 132–4

kinds of involvement 93–4
knowledge 141

'ladder of citizen
participation' 48
land use issues 7, 66
language 84–5, 174
equal opportunities 75–7
information-gathering and
consultation 36
records 168–9
lay advocacy 88, 209
see also citizen advocacy
leaders 148–9
learning and involvement 66,
68
learning difficulties, people
with 92, 182–3, 188, 190,
192
advisers 121
advocacy 90
citizenship 4–5
confidence-building 55–6,
58
democratic model 9

empowerment of 133, 134, 135, 148
equal opportunities 78–9
information-gathering and consultation 29–30
listening to 161
relating to 193
research by 72
rights of 169
self-advocacy 57
social role valorisation 3
social services 13
training of 68, 71
legal action 116
legal advocacy 87, 209
legal rights 4, 164
legislation for involvement 199
levels of involvement 212
limited mobility, people with 75
limits of involvement 96–7, 118, 198
listening 26–7, 29–30, 137, 160–1
lobbying 116
local government
constraints on 7
forums 81

managing of agencies 11
manipulation 124–5
marginalisation 125, 126, 151, 153
market economy 8
market research 23, 43
material support 51–2, 54, 210
meetings
drawbacks of 106
information-gathering and consultation 25
mental health distress *see* people with mental health distress

minority ethnic
communities *see* ethnic minorities, members of
monitoring
information-gathering and consultation 40, 104
social services 188
multi-racial communities 76
mutual aid 116, 118, 152

National Consumer Council 43
National Health Service 43
nature of involvement 109–11, 205
needs assessment 24, 45
negotiation 116, 134–6, 147, 162, 194
newcomers, inclusion of 138–9, 195
non-statutory organisations 81
normalisation 3, 188–9
nurseries 95–6, 110
training 67

objectives, agency 205–6
obligations, citizenship 4
official information 67
older people 186–7
accommodation 195
forums 82
racism 110
reminiscence work 112
rural areas 196
safeguards 98–9
self-confidence 57, 58–9
social services 13
support for 53
open-endedness of involvement 107–8
open groups 80
opinion polls 23

opportunities for
 involvement 51, 210–11
opposition
 to empowerment 148–9
 to involvement 16–17
opting out of schools 8
organising 15, 119–20

parents 92, 159, 170–1
 access to records 168
 communication 110
 complaints procedures 166
 information 65
 negotiation 135
 research 74
 rights 174–5
 and schools 8
 social services 13
 support of 62
participation
 community 3, 4
 history of 7, 21, 50
 initiatives 15, 39–41, 52, 56
 policies of 2, 43, 52, 56
 profile of 205, 207–8
participatory research 98
paternalism 17, 20
 community
  development 123–7
peer advocacy 88, 209
peer counselling 152
people with HIV/AIDS 162,
  178, 187–8
 counselling of 158
 forums 81
 rights of 167
 self-help groups 59, 152
people with mental distress
 choice of
  involvement 108–9
 empowerment of 133, 135,
  148, 159, 175
 forums 80, 143–4
 relating to 193

research by 72–3, 74
 self-confidence of 57
 steering committees 95
 support of 62, 126
 training of 69
performance-related pay 180
personal aspects of
 involvement 52
personal change for
 involvement 15, 54
personal concerns and group
 discussions 33
personal dealings with
 agencies 11
personal development 192–3
personal effect of
 involvement 1–2
personal support 51–2, 54,
  208–9
philosophies supporting
 involvement 3
physical access to
 buildings 75, 99
pilot surveys 32
planning, involvement in 11
play centres 191
policies
 development procedures 18
 for involvement 205,
  214–15
 involvement in 11
political change 192–3
political rights 4
politicisation 118
politics
 and citizenship 4
 of disability 3
 opinion polls 23
 of participation 2, 43, 52,
  60–1
poor people 53
 citizenship 4
 forums 145–6
 language 85

positive approaches 30–1, 43, 197
potential use of agencies 207
practice
  agency 205, 213–14
  empowerment 157–76
prerequisites for
  participation 205, 208–11
presence, community 3
pressures
  against
    empowerment 148–9
  for involvement 8
preventive services 173
principles for
  empowerment 160–3
privatisation 8
pro-active access policy 167–8
pro-active involvement 12, 185
problems
  community
    development 117–20
  information-gathering and
    consultation 37–8, 42–8
process
  of empowerment 130–6
  of involvement 15, 60–1, 202
professional advocacy 87–8, 89, 209
  rights 164–5
professionalisation 21, 193
professionals, working
  with 142–3
profile of participants 205, 207–8
profiling, community 24
programmes, consultation 39
protection
  effectiveness of 49–50
  of social workers 175
provision for minority ethnic
  communities 104–5

psychiatric services, recipients
  of
  identity 151
  information 66
  manipulation of 124
  safeguards 98
  treatment of 162–3
psychological access 75
public advocacy 88
public service
  organisations 44
publicity and public
  consultation 43

qualitative information 24
quality action groups 28
quality circles 28, 44
quality control 187–8, 194–5
quantitative information 24
questionnaires 27, 34, 37

racism 115
reaching people 36–7, 39, 185
reactive involvement 12
realism and community
  development 121
reciprocity 163
records, access to 167–70, 184–6
recruitment policies 77, 194
redevelopment of land 7
redress 201
refugees
  credibility of views 111
  equal access 78
  and social workers 163
refusals, survey 37
regulation issues 14
relationships, building of 137, 176, 193–4
reluctance for
  involvement 16–17, 43–4, 80, 150
reminiscence work 112

representation 149–50, 184,
    201
  objections to
    involvement 18–19
research
  for involvement 72–4
  participatory 98
researchers 72–4
reserved places 106
residential services 186–7
resources
  availability of 97
  rural areas 196
  support of involvement 52,
    61–3, 140, 214–16
  training 69–70
responsibility 9–10, 21
results of consultation
  feeding back of 33-4, 40
  use of 38–40
rights
  advocacy 89
  of children 79
  citizenship 4
  and empowerment 164–71
  of older people 186
  organisations 15
  protection of 3, 97–100,
    212–13
  restriction of 13–14, 174–5
risk factor 14
roles, valued 3
routes to involvement 15–16
running of agencies 11
rural dwellers 195–6

safeguards 97–100, 214
sampling 37
  continuous 28
satisfaction surveys 46
scale of involvement 119
scepticism 98, 174
  information-gathering and
    consultation 43, 44

schools 8, 198–9
search conferences 28, 44
  languages 84
secure accommodation 145
self-advocacy 56–9, 85–7, 89,
    114–15, 209
  community
    development 120,
    121–3
  empowerment 148, 149
  groups 74
  negotiation 135
  objections to 176
  people with learning
    difficulties 183
  rights to 164–5
self confidence 55–9
  see also confidence-building
self-esteem 55–6, 57
self-help groups 152
  allies 123
  control 10
  parents of children in
    care 159
  participatory initiatives 15
  people with HIV/AIDS 59
  service culture 4
self-operated support
    schemes 152
sensory disabilities, people
    with 76, 78–9
separatist groups 80
service brokerage 87
service culture 4–6
service intervention 14–15
service sampling 193
services
  decentralisation of 3
  information required 64
  involvement in 11
  kinds of 3
  providers and users 193–4,
    196
  rights to 164

settings for involvement 53, 128, 129–30
  social services 173
sign language 76
single parents 55
single voice, desire for 148–9
skills for involvement 51–2, 63, 68, 144
  and rights 165
  sharing of 141–2
social administration 5
social control 14
Social Fund 90
social rights 4
social role valorisation 3, 188–9
social security
  claimants' commission 62
  problems 159–60
social services
  continuity 103–4
  differences 12–13
  equal opportunities 77–8, 79
  forums 80–1
  language 84–5
  marginalisation of involvement 126
  people with HIV/AIDS 188
  problems 53
  reorganisation of 177
  stigma and dependency 172–3
  training 70–1
social workers 163
  access to records 167–8, 169–70, 185–6
  advocacy 90
  equal opportunities 77
  goals 101
  power of 13–14, 159
  training 71–2
  violence towards 173–4
starting involvement 94–6, 216

state 5, 14–15
statutory organisations 81
stigma 172–3
structures for involvement 15, 51, 79–83
students 142
success of involvement 19
supplementary benefit tribunals
  advocacy 90
  informality of 106
support
  for advisers 122
  for community development 119–20, 121, 124
  for empowerment 133, 137, 146, 150, 162
  for involvement 19–20, 51–4, 62, 109
  in involvement policy 187, 208–10
  and rights 165
  for workers 173, 175–6
support services 5
supporters 72
surveys 24, 25, 27
  bias 37
  satisfaction 46
  social services 188
systems, workings of 38

taking over of participants 125–6
talents 3
targeting people
  equal opportunities 77
  information-gathering and consultation 39
teamwork 136–7, 180
tenants
  community development 127
  forums 80

tenants (*cont.*)
  housing improvements 65,
    103
  training 68, 69–70, 71
therapeutic benefits of
    empowerment 109
timing and equality 75
tokenism
  avoidance of 125
  consultation 48
  equal opportunities 105
  of involvement 171
top–down initiatives 190–2
training for
    involvement 67–72, 145,
    198–9
  policy 183, 185, 188, 194
tranquillizers, information
    on 66–7
translators 77
  see also interpreters
transport 195–6
tribunals
  advocacy 90, 165
  informality of 106
trusts, establishment of 152
two-way training 69

undermining of
    participants 125–6
unemployed people 111
use of agencies 207
use of information 38–40
user groups
  allies 123
  empowerment of 128–9
  representation problems 19
  setting up of 80, 118
  support of 62, 124–5
  training of 69
'user' term 85, 110, 151
users' charters 98, 164

value placed on people 19, 26
valued roles 3
violence 173–4
voluntary organisations 196
  and advocacy 90
  control 9–10
  forums 81
voyeurism 125

welfare advisory
    committees 43
welfare state
  disenchantment with 2
  run-down of 7
  service culture 4–6
whole person concept 162–3
women
  citizenship 4
  discrimination 108
  equal opportunities 4, 75
  information-gathering and
    consultation 37
  language 84, 85
  self-confidence 58–9
  and social workers 163
  transport 195
women's organisations
  changing attitudes 194
  forums 145–6
  self-confidence 58–9
workers, empowerment
    of 175–6, 214
working together 136–7

young people
  data protection 167
  with mental distress 72–3
  reciprocity 163
  unemployed 111
  see also care, young people in;
    children
youth centres 102